MAPS of the WORLD

An ILLUSTRATED CHILDREN'S ATLAS of ADVENTURE, CULTURE, and DISCOVERY

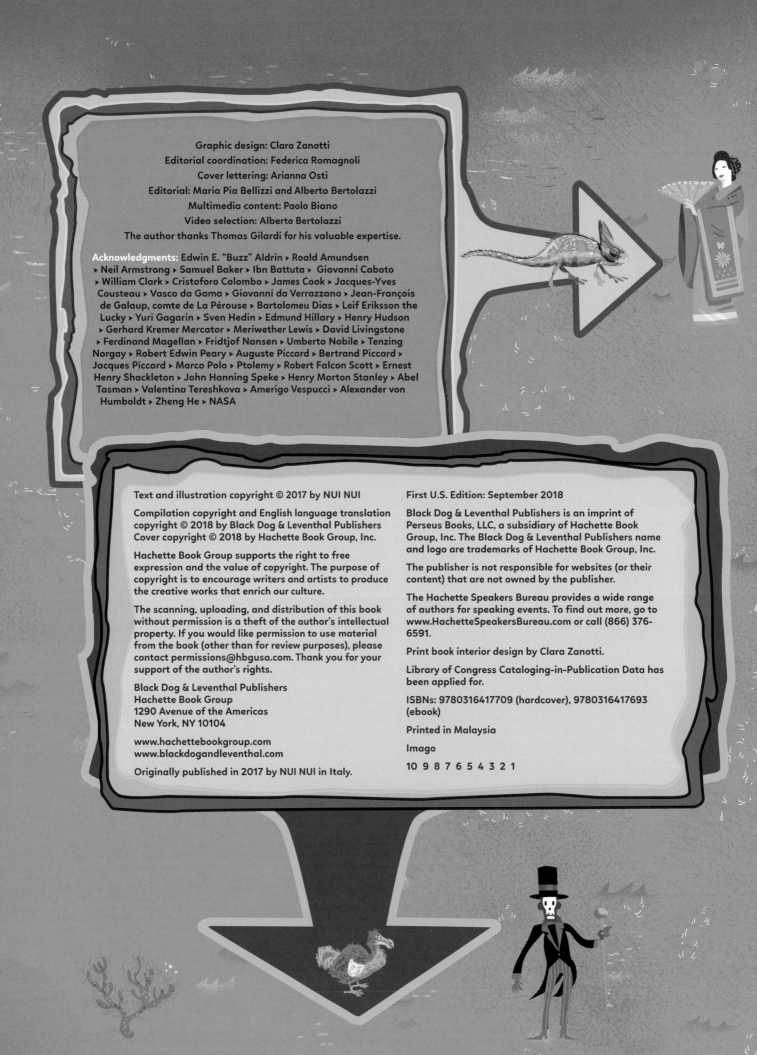

Graphic design: Clara Zanotti
Editorial coordination: Federica Romagnoli
Cover lettering: Arianna Osti
Editorial: Maria Pia Bellizzi and Alberto Bertolazzi
Multimedia content: Paolo Biano
Video selection: Alberto Bertolazzi
The author thanks Thomas Gilardi for his valuable expertise.

Acknowledgments: Edwin E. "Buzz" Aldrin ▸ Roald Amundsen ▸ Neil Armstrong ▸ Samuel Baker ▸ Ibn Battuta ▸ Giovanni Caboto ▸ William Clark ▸ Cristoforo Colombo ▸ James Cook ▸ Jacques-Yves Cousteau ▸ Vasco da Gama ▸ Giovanni da Verrazzano ▸ Jean-François de Galaup, comte de La Pérouse ▸ Bartolomeu Dias ▸ Leif Eriksson the Lucky ▸ Yuri Gagarin ▸ Sven Hedin ▸ Edmund Hillary ▸ Henry Hudson ▸ Gerhard Kremer Mercator ▸ Meriwether Lewis ▸ David Livingstone ▸ Ferdinand Magellan ▸ Fridtjof Nansen ▸ Umberto Nobile ▸ Tenzing Norgay ▸ Robert Edwin Peary ▸ Auguste Piccard ▸ Bertrand Piccard ▸ Jacques Piccard ▸ Marco Polo ▸ Ptolemy ▸ Robert Falcon Scott ▸ Ernest Henry Shackleton ▸ John Hanning Speke ▸ Henry Morton Stanley ▸ Abel Tasman ▸ Valentina Tereshkova ▸ Amerigo Vespucci ▸ Alexander von Humboldt ▸ Zheng He ▸ NASA

First U.S. Edition: September 2018

Black Dog & Leventhal Publishers is an imprint of Perseus Books, LLC, a subsidiary of Hachette Book Group, Inc. The Black Dog & Leventhal Publishers name and logo are trademarks of Hachette Book Group, Inc.

The publisher is not responsible for websites (or their content) that are not owned by the publisher.

The Hachette Speakers Bureau provides a wide range of authors for speaking events. To find out more, go to www.HachetteSpeakersBureau.com or call (866) 376-6591.

Print book interior design by Clara Zanotti.

Library of Congress Cataloging-in-Publication Data has been applied for.

ISBNs: 9780316417709 (hardcover), 9780316417693 (ebook)

Printed in Malaysia

Imago

10 9 8 7 6 5 4 3 2 1

MAPS of the WORLD

An ILLUSTRATED CHILDREN'S ATLAS of ADVENTURE, CULTURE, and DISCOVERY

Text by
Enrico Lavagno

Illustrations by
Sacco and Vallarino

BLACK DOG
& LEVENTHAL
PUBLISHERS
NEW YORK

Contents

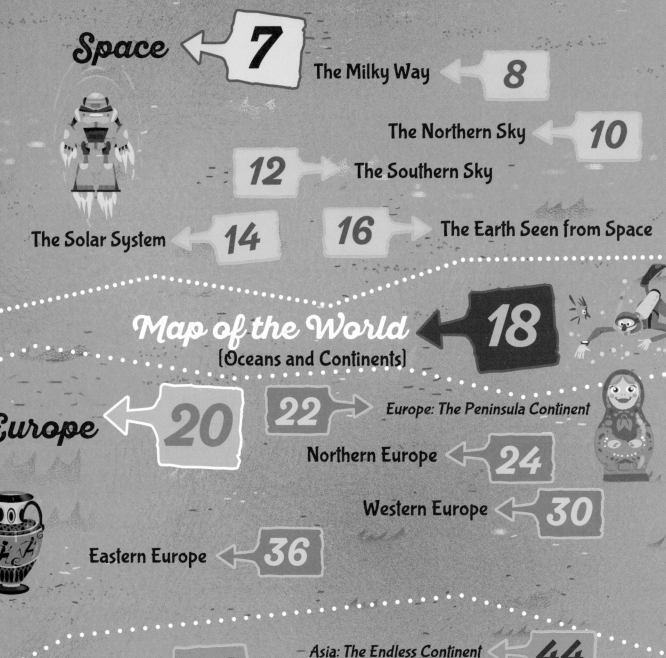

Nebula

The nebula is one of the largest structures in the universe: It's a cloud of dust and gas (mostly hydrogen and helium) that floats in deep space. These clouds come in various shapes and sizes and are millions of light years long. When the gases and dust inside a nebula collide, they create stars.

Space

The Milky Way

Our home within the universe is really big. It's called a galaxy and is made of billions of stars like the Sun. The stars create a great big band of light as white as milk that can be seen in the dark night sky. That's why our galaxy is called the Milky Way.

The Milky Way is so enormous that we need special measurements like light—years to figure out how large it is. Let's say that light, which travels faster than any other thing in the universe, takes more than 100,000 years to get from the tip of one of the galaxy's spiral arms to the tip of the one on the opposite side. This means when we look at a star that's in another part of the galaxy, the light we see coming from it was first released all the way back when our species had only just evolved on Earth.

The Milky Way is a spiral galaxy. This means that it has a center (the "galactic nucleus") and spiral "arms" that stretch into space. The Earth is in one of these spiral arms, called the Orion Arm, on the outer edge of the galaxy.

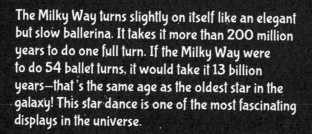

The Milky Way turns slightly on itself like an elegant but slow ballerina. It takes it more than 200 million years to do one full turn. If the Milky Way were to do 54 ballet turns, it would take it 13 billion years—that's the same age as the oldest star in the galaxy! This star dance is one of the most fascinating displays in the universe.

The Northern Sky

If you look at the sky on a moonless night, it can seem like we are in the middle of a dome decorated on the inside with thousands of stars. There are two of these "domes": one of them is visible from the Northern Hemisphere

(or Boreal Hemisphere),

and the other is visible from the Southern Hemisphere

(or Austral Hemisphere).

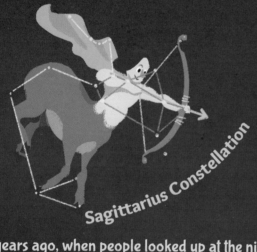

Sagittarius Constellation

Many years ago, when people looked up at the night sky, they saw that some of the stars seemed to form shapes. They added imaginary lines between the stars to create pictures in the sky. These are called *constellations*.

Ursa Major

Orion Constellation

Researchers found a mammoth bone from 32,000 years ago with what looks like the Orion constellation drawn on it. That means people have been looking at constellations for a very long time. Orion is named after a hunter in Greek mythology.

AQUARIUS

PEGASUS

EQUULEUS

DELPHINUS

VULPECULA

AQUILA

SAGITTA

CYGNUS

SERPENS

LYRA

DRACO

OPHIUCHUS

HERCULES

CORONA BOREALIS

SERPENS

BOÖTES

COMA BERENICES

The Cassiopeia constellation is named after a vain, mythical queen. It has five stars that together create an M spread across the Milky Way.

Cassiopeia Constellation

Centaurus Constellation

CETUS

ARIES

TRIANGULUM

ANDROMEDA

LACERTA

CASSIOPEIA

CEPHEUS

CAMELOPARDIS

TAURUS

PERSEUS

ORION

AURIGA

NORTH STAR

URSA MINOR

LYNX

GEMINI

CANIS MINOR

URSA MAJOR

CANCER

CANES VENATICI

LEO MINOR

HYDRA

LEO

VIRGO

The constellations may seem close together, but they are actually far away from each other in space. For example, in the Centaurus constellation shines a star called Proxima Centauri that is 4.5 light-years away from us. The constellation called Hydra includes the Messier 83 (or Southern Pinwheel Galaxy), which seems close to Proxima Centauri when you look at them from Earth, but Hydra is in a galaxy 15 million light-years away from us.

The Southern Sky

Because we can't feel the Earth rotating, it can seem like the constellations move around in the sky. They actually stay in the same position in relation to each other, but as the Earth makes the same turn each day, it looks like they're revolving around us. It's this constant rotation that makes star charts so useful.

Thanks to constellation maps, what looks like a mess of distant stars is transformed into a map full of landmarks. For example, if we are in the ocean, or in the middle of the desert, or even deep in space, the maps allow us to point our telescopes toward a specific area of the universe and know exactly where we are.

CETUS

ERIDANUS

FORNAX

CAELUM

RETICU

DORADO

ORION

LEPUS

COLUMBA

PICTOR

MONOCEROS

CANIS MAJOR

CARINA

PUPPIS

VE

PYXIS

ANTLIA

SEXTANS

Star charts can be even more useful than normal land maps because they help us know our position not only in space, but also in time. This makes them very helpful for farming, space navigation, and astronomy.

The Solar System

Earth and the planets around it are part of the solar system, which is in the Milky Way. Scientists believe that 4.5 billion years ago a cloud of dust and gas started to collapse, and the matter within the cloud started moving around in a giant circle. As the cloud kept spinning, other clumps of dust and gas created the Sun and the planets surrounding it.

Sun

TEMPERATURE: -130–806°F
(-90–430°C)
DISTANCE FROM THE SUN:
36 MILLION MILES
(58 MILLION KM)

Mercury

TEMPERATURE: -76–131°F
(-60–55°C)
DISTANCE FROM THE SUN:
93 MILLION MILES
(150 MILLION KM)

Earth

Venus

TEMPERATURE: 860°F
(460°C)
DISTANCE FROM THE SUN:
67 MILLION MILES
(108 MILLION KM)

Mars

TEMPERATURE: -220–-68°F
(-140–20°C)
DISTANCE FROM THE SUN:
142 MILLION MILES
(228 MILLION KM)

Jupiter

TEMPERATURE: -418°F (-250°C)
DISTANCE FROM THE SUN: 485 MILLION MILES (780 MILLION KM)

Earth is the third planet from the Sun. That's a great spot to be in because it means we are in the Goldilocks zone: a narrow area in space where it's possible for life to exist on planets.

The Earth has been rotating around the Sun for 4.5 billion years, since the creation of the solar system. The Sun is actually a small star compared to other stars in the universe. It's classified as a "yellow dwarf" star and is 93 million miles (150 million km) away.

depth 1740 miles (2900 km)
temperature 1600–4000°F
(870–2200°C)
MANTLE

CRUST depth 25 miles (40 km)
temperature 77–1598°F (25–870°C)

OUTER CORE
depth 1367 miles (2200 km)
temperature 4000–16232°F
(2200–9000°C)

INNER CORE
depth 1367 miles (2200 km)
temperature 9752°F (5400°C)

Saturn TEMPERATURE: -292°F (-180°C)
DISTANCE FROM THE SUN: 889 MILLION MILES (1.4 BILLION KM)

Uranus
TEMPERATURE: -364°F (-220°C)
DISTANCE FROM THE SUN:
1.8 BILLION MILES
(2.9 BILLION KM)

Neptune
TEMPERATURE: -364°F (-220°C)
DISTANCE FROM THE SUN:
2.8 BILLION MILES (4.5 BILLION KM)

If the Sun were a basketball on the ground, the Earth would be an apple seed on top of a 12-story palace (80 ft/24 m).

If the Earth were 1 year old, humans would have existed for 1 minute and 10 seconds.

One reason life exists on Earth is because of what's inside of it. Underneath the Earth's surface, or crust, which is what we live on, the planet saves the heat that has been building up for billions of years since the Earth was formed.

Inside the inner core, 3,700 miles (6,000 km) deep, the temperature rises to 9752°F (5400°C). Without this warm core, the Earth would be like Mars: lifeless and cold. The Earth's core is full of molten iron that creates a large magnetic field which protects the planet like an umbrella. Without it, meteorites would rain down on the Earth all the time.

The Earth Seen from Space

We have all seen photographs of Earth from space, thanks to satellites that go around the world. Yet only astronauts have been able to admire it with their own eyes.

When looking at our planet from the side, against the blackness of deep space, you can see a thin film surrounding it like a bubble. This is the atmosphere. Its bottom layer is composed of the air we breathe.

The atmosphere is also where meteorological phenomena, or the weather, happens. The clouds we can see from space are caused by the evaporation of the oceans as part of the water cycle. The Sun heats water in the lakes and oceans around the world, which makes them evaporate, or turn from water to gas, and rise into the sky. When this vapor rises into the atmosphere, it cools and creates the cloud systems that are blown across the surface of the planet by the wind.

You can see everything from space! It's how we know there is three times more water on Earth than there is land, and that the mountain chains are all linked together like the stitching on a baseball.

Thanks to the infinite cycle of evaporation, condensation, and rainfall, we are able to live on planet Earth. The color of the land depends on the quantity of rain: the sandy Sahara and Arabian deserts don't get much rain and therefore shine yellow, while South Asia and the Amazon are green with humid tropical forests.

The Earth seen from space is always beautiful, most of all when it turns from day to night by turning on its axis. As the shadows draw nearer, the night face of the planet lights up, revealing its big cities and the communication lines that connect them.

The oceans and the uninhabited territories, on the other hand, look completely dark, showing the separation between space occupied by humans and space occupied by nature.

North
America

Central
America

Pacific Ocean

Atlantic
Ocean

Map
of the
World

South
America

Atlantic
Ocean

North Pole

Norwegian Sea

Europe

Asia

Africa

Pacific Ocean

Indian Ocean

Oceania

South Pole

Antarctica

Europe

Population:
737 million

Surface area:
3.86 million square miles
(10 million km²)

Link to download the map:
https://www.hachettebookgroup.com/europe

ICELAND

Svalbard (NORWAY)

Norwegian Sea

Faroe Islands (DENMARK)

Shetland Islands (UK)

NORWAY

SWED

North Sea

DENMARK

IRELAND

UNITED KINGDOM

NETHERLANDS

BELGIUM

GERMANY

LUXEMBOURG

CZECH REP

FRANCE

LIECHTENSTEIN

SWITZERLAND

AUSTRIA

SLOVENIA

CRO

Azores (PORTUGAL)

Atlantic Ocean

ITALY

PORTUGAL

ANDORRA

PRINCIPALITY
OF MONACO

SAN
MARINO

SPAIN

VATICAN
CITY

Mediterranean Sea

MALTA

Barents
Sea

FINLAND

Baltic Sea

ESTONIA

LATVIA

LITHUANIA

Kaliningrad
Oblast
(RUSSIA)

BELARUS

POLAND

UKRAINE

SLOVAKIA

MOLDOVA

HUNGARY

ROMANIA

AND
OVINA

SERBIA

Black Sea

MONTENEGRO

KOSOVO

BULGARIA

MACEDONIA

TURKEY

ALBANIA

GREECE

CYPRUS

RUSSIA

Caspian Sea

21

Europe
The Peninsula Continent

Europe is really a small peninsula, which is a body of land surrounded by water on three sides. It is part of the supercontinent Eurasia, which extends to the borders of the Middle East, China, and India.

Europe began to rise out of the sea 400 million years ago in the form of islands and mountains like the Alps and Great Britain's Grampian Mountains.

Europe is surrounded by several seas: the Atlantic Ocean to the west, the North Sea, Norwegian Sea, Barents Sea, and the Baltic Sea to the north, the Mediterranean to the south, and the Black Sea to the east. They help keep Europe's temperature mild by bringing rain and lowering the temperature.

The highest mountains in Europe, like Mont Blanc in the Alps (15,781 feet/4,810 m) and the Aneto in the Pyrenees (11,168 feet/3,404 m) are part of mountain chains that are still growing.

These mountains create large rivers that supply water to most of Europe. The Danube river runs for 1,780 miles (2,860 km) in the east through 9 countries. The Rhône is 505 miles (813 km) long and brings humidity to the hot South of France. The Rhine flows into the North Sea after having soaked 760 miles (1,230 km) of land in Austria, Switzerland, France, and Germany.

Thanks to these rivers, Europe is the only continent without big deserts. Farmland, woodland, forests, and grassland cover almost all of it, from Norway to Italy and from Portugal to Ukraine.

Today, most of the animals living in Europe are farm animals. There are many cows, pigs, and sheep.

However, in the mountains like the Carpathians, the Pyrenees, and the Alps, and in the big forests like the Black Forest in Germany, there are still some wild animals like bears, wolves, chamois, bison, and rare birds such as the greater spotted eagle.

The different temperatures and currents of the numerous seas around Europe determine which kinds of animals live there. The ocean is full of oily fish like sardines and many marine mammals such as whales and dolphins that live in the Mediterranean.

Scientists believe that modern humans started to arrive in Europe from the Middle East about 35,000 years ago. Some early settlers created magnificent rock paintings they left in Spain and France.

The mild climate makes farming and animal raising possible in almost the entire continent. Some typical European crops are olive trees and grapevines near the Mediterranean and grains and vegetables in the east.

On the other hand, mineral resources are becoming scarce, except for coal. Coal started the industrial revolution in Europe 300 years ago. Today coal is mainly mined in Poland.

Thanks to trains, industrial machines, engines, and electricity, Europe became an industrialized continent 200 years ago.

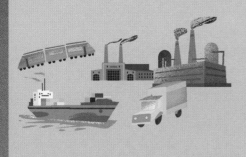

There are currently more than 200 languages and dialects spoken in Europe. More than 700 million people live on the continent and most of them are in the big cities (61 of which have more than a million inhabitants) and in industrial zones like the Ruhr in Germany and the Upper Silesian Industrial Region in Poland.

Europe is no longer the economic power it used to be, but is very active in the chemical and pharmaceutical industries and in services like transport, communications, and tourism.

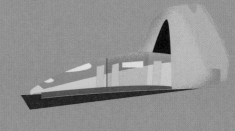

Food is particularly rich, as it reflects the traditions of many populations, but it's the most simple dishes that have conquered the world. Italy's pizza, Belgium's fries, Spain's paella, and Germany and Austria's würst are just a few examples. Many regions in Europe produce wine, beer, cheese, and excellent pastries.

Europe is home to beautiful beaches on the Mediterranean sea, unique cities like Venice, and modern architecture like the fantastic Basilica of the Sagrada Familia in Barcelona.

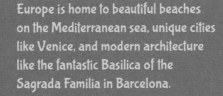

European civilizations have left important architecture behind. Stonehenge in England was built 5,000 years ago, the Colosseum in Rome was built 2,000 years ago, plus there are cathedrals and medieval castles all over the continent. There are also important monuments like the Brandenburg Gate in Berlin, which was built in 1791, and the Eiffel Tower in Paris, which was built in 1889.

Northern Europe

Atlantic Ocean

Reykjavik

ICELAND

Faroe Islands (DENMARK)

Link to download the map:

https://www.hachettebookgroup.com/northern-europe

UNITED KINGDOM

IRELAND

Dublin

London

North Sea

007

North Cape

Barents
Sea

FINLAND

SWEDEN

Helsinki ✦

NORWAY   Oslo ✦

Stockholm ✦

Tallinn ✦

ESTONIA

Baltic Sea

DENMARK

Riga ✦

LATVIA

LITHUANIA

Copenhagen ✦

Vilnius ✦

25

Northern Europe

Iceland

The **Hallgrímskirkja** in Reykjavík is a Lutheran church that took 41 years to build! It is the second highest building in Iceland.

The **giant squid** lives in the cold waters of the North Atlantic Ocean and can grow up to 43 feet (13 m) long.

For centuries, Denmark's economy was mainly **fishing**.

The island has approximately 130 **active volcanos**. Most of them erupt every 10 years.

The brain of the sperm whale, the biggest creature in the animal kingdom, can weigh up to 22 pounds (10 kg).

You can visit **Viking warships**, which were 90 feet (30 m) long and could fit 70 crew members, at a museum in Roskilde.

The oldest **Icelandic geyser** is called Geysir and spouts boiling water up to 180 feet (60 m) in the air.

Denmark

Edvard Eriksen, the sculptor who created the statue in Copenhagen called **The Little Mermaid**, used his wife as a model for the body and a ballerina for the face.

Norway

The Nobel Peace prize award ceremony is held in **Oslo City Hall**.

One of the first **Vikings** to reach Iceland was the Norseman Naddodd, who named it Snowland.

Each day at noon the **Royal Guard** crosses Copenhagen from Rosenborg Castle to the Royal Amalienborg Palace.

Norway is full off **dense conifer forests**.

The **dragon** is considered one of the four protectors of the country. According to legend, it watches over the northeastern part of the island.

Hamlet, a famous play by British playwright William Shakespeare, is set in Kronborg Castle in Helsingør.

A **moose**'s horns can grow up to 4.5 feet (1.5 m) long.

The **Icelandic horse** is about 4.5 feet (1.5 m) high and is similar to a pony.

In the **Legoland Billund** theme park, kids can drive electric cars that look like they are made of Legos.

According to Norwegian legend, **trolls**, the mythical creatures of the forest, cannot stand the sound of bells.

Herring is a type of fish that's very popular in Iceland.

At the Fanø International Kite Festival, millions of **kites** fly over the white beaches of the island.

Stave churches, typical Norwegian medieval churches built of wood, are decorated with delicately carved designs inspired by Christian ideas, dragons, and animals.

Back in the 9th century, the Vikings were already using *sleds* very similar to those used today in competitions.

The *Sami knife* is a jewel of Sami handicraft. The handle is made of layers of birch and horn.

Reindeer are raised in Scandinavia for meat, leather, milk, and their *antlers*. They are also used as transportation.

"*Ski*" comes from the Norwegian word skíð which means "a piece of wood."

Ski jumping was born in Norway and spread through all of Scandinavia and the Alpine countries.

You can find *brown bears* in some parts of Scandinavian forests. They can weigh more than 881 pounds (400 kg).

Fictional sea *monsters* that terrified the sailors in the north often looked like dragons or serpents.

Queen Margaret I lived in *Kalmar Castle* in 1397 and ruled over Denmark, Sweden, and Norway.

Pine, fir, and birch trees grow in *Finnish forests*.

The *orca*, which is a kind of whale that lives in practically every sea in the world, can grow up to 27 feet (9 m) long and weigh up to 10 tons.

Pippi Longstocking, a famous book and TV character, lived alone in Visby, on the island of Gotland.

Many people think *Santa's* home is in the Lappish city of Rovaniemi.

Sweden

The Nobel Prize award banquet, or fancy dinner, takes place in *Stockholm City Hall*.

The *Vasa* was a war ship that sank in the port of Stockholm on the same day it was launched, on August 10, 1628.

Ice hockey is Finland's national sport and the most popular in Scandinavia.

In the north of Sweden, *reindeer* are used to pull *pulks*, traditional Scandinavian sleds.

The winners of the Nobel Prize receive a *gold medal* that with Alfred Nobel's face on it. He invented dynamite.

Kayaking is very popular in Finland.

A *Dalecarlian horse* is a typical Swedish wooden statue. The biggest one in the world is 40 feet (13 m) high and can be found in the town of Avesta.

Finland

The *Helsinki Cathedral* was finished in 1852.

According to mythology, gnomes live in *Finnish saunas* and should be treated with respect.

The traditional *Sami tent*, used by a group of people who live in Lapland called the Sami people, is a portable tent made of reindeer hide.

The colors of the *gákti*, the traditional clothing of Finland, are the same as those of the Sami flag.

The *dogs* most often used for pulling *sleds* are the Husky, Samoyed, and Malamute breeds.

Lithuania

It's said that a magic tile at the base of the steeple of *Vilnius Cathedral* grants all wishes.

Many Lithuanian dishes are based around one ingredient that is by far the most common ingredient in the Baltic: *dried herring*.

On the *Hill of Crosses*, in Šiauliai, there are over 100,000 crosses, planted by pilgrims.

The most popular sport in Lithuania is *basketball*, which is played by half of the population.

Latvia

The *Freedom Monument* in Riga is loved by the Latvians, who regularly leave flowers at its feet.

A branch of the so-called *Friendship Pipeline*, the longest oil pipeline in the world, runs through Ventspils.

Latvia is covered in extensive forests inhabited by *lynxes*, now extremely rare in the rest of Europe.

Like in Lithuania, in Latvia the tradition of *ceramic* production dates back to at least the 16th century.

Estonia

St Olaf's Church in Tallinn, whose steeple was originally 522 feet (159 m) high, but was cut down to 407 feet (124 m) during the 19th century restoration, was the highest building in Europe for a long time.

The *Hermann Castle and Ivangorod Fortress*, separated by the Narva river, defend the Estonian and Russian borders.

The traditional wooden *windmill* is considered to be the symbol of the island of Saaremaa.

You can see a beautiful view of the castle and of the whole city from the *Viljandi Old Water Tower*.

The *swallow* is the Estonians' favorite animal, which they see as a symbol of freedom and happiness.

United Kingdom (Great Britain)

The *British rail network* is one of the oldest in the world but at the same time one of the most modern ones.

The Clock Tower in Westminster is nicknamed *Big Ben* for the size of its bell.

Queen Elizabeth II has ruled the British monarchy, one of the most ancient, since 1952.

The big stones that make up the Neolithic site *Stonehenge* can way up to 25 tons each.

The *Artognou (or Arthur) stone* was found in Cornwall in 1998. Some people think it's associated with King Arthur.

After the USA, Great Britain was the birthplace of *rock and roll*, in the decade between 1958 and 1969.

Winchester Cathedral, founded in the 7th century, is one of the oldest Benedictine monasteries.

The *typical rural cottage* is built of stone or bricks and sometimes has a thatched roof.

Shakespeare, the most famous English writer, is considered one of the "fathers" of the British nation.

The *Rolls-Royce*, owned today by BMW, was the symbol of the English automotive industry for many years.

The adventures of *Robin Hood* are set in Sherwood Forest in Nottinghamshire.

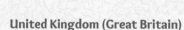

Some **windmills** that are left over from the Middle Ages can still be seen in the English countryside.

 James Bond, the famous fictional **007 agent**, was created in the 1950s by the British writer Ian Fleming.

 Ireland

 According to the legend, the sound from the **celtic harp** allowed the wizard Merlin to levitate rocks.

 The city of Manchester is truly the capital of **English football (soccer)**. It has two historic, winning teams.

 British author Sir Arthur Conan Doyle created the fictional private detective **Sherlock Holmes** in 1887. Holmes is one of the most famous characters in history.

 The medieval **Dunluce Castle** was abandoned centuries ago but it is still a symbol of Ireland.

 The **modern industrial revolution** began here, at the heart of England, to the east of Wales.

 The **Arctic puffin**, with its comical looking face, lives on the Northern Atlantic coasts.

 Guinness, a dark colored beer, has been produced in Ireland since 1759.

 The little **Yorkshire Terrier** dogs were once used to catch mice in factories and mines.

 Both **rugby** and modern **football (soccer)** were born in British schools around the middle of the 19th century.

 The **Celtic cross** has been a symbol of Ireland since the 9th century.

 Scafell Pike, the highest mountain in England, is part of the **Lake District National Park**.

 The coast of Great Britain is protected by a **lighthouse** system. Some are still active; others have been turned into guesthouses.

 Suffolk sheep are very wooly and can weigh up to 264 pounds (120 kg).

 Edinburgh Castle was built on an extinct volcano.

 Dolphins are common in the cold waters of the North Atlantic, where they find food easily.

 Foxes aren't always red. They can range from pale yellow to reddish brown.

 Highland cattle live in high altitude even in the cold season, like Tibetan yaks.

 Scotland has over 31,000 miles (50,000 km) of rivers. Many of them are home to wild Atlantic **salmon** and sea trout.

 Glendalough Round Tower, in County Wicklow, was built during the years of the Viking invasions to safeguard the relics of Saint Kevin.

 The **kilt** and **whisky** are two symbols that famously represent Scotland throughout the world.

 The **sperm whale** gets its name from the oily, waxy liquid contained inside its head.

 European lobsters are blue but turn red when they are cooked.

 The first person to spot the legendary **Loch Ness Monster** was a monk in 565, which he wrote about in his memoirs.

 More than half of the oil extracted in Europe comes from the big **platforms** in the North Sea.

Western Europe

Link to download the map:

https://www.hachettebookgroup.com/western-europe

Atlantic Ocean

English

Lisbon

PORTUGAL

PORTO

Madrid

SPAIN

Strait of Gibraltar

North Sea

*Amsterdam
NETHERLANDS

*Berlin

GERMANY

TINTIN

*Brussels
BELGIUM

LUXEMBOURG

*LUXEMBOURG

Paris *

Vienna *

LIECHTENSTEIN
*Vaduz

AUSTRIA

RANCE

*Bern
SWITZERLAND

PRINCIPALITY
OF MONACO

*Monaco

SAN
MARINO

DORRA

ndorra
Vella

ITALY

Islands (SPAIN)

Adriatic Sea

Corsica

Rome *

VATICAN
CITY

Sardinia

Tyrrhenian Sea

Ionian Sea

Mediterranean Sea

Sicily

MALTA

*Valletta

31

Western Europe

Portugal

The **Rooster of Barcelos** is a figure in Portuguese folklore and is a symbol of honesty, trust, and honor.

The typical Spanish **guitar** is called the flamenco guitar. It's smaller and lighter than a classical guitar and has a very bright sound.

The Spanish **road network** of highways and fast roads is more than 9,940 miles (16,000 km) long.

The **Iberian wolf** (Canis lupus signatus) lives in northern Portugal and gets its name from its streaked coat.

Cattle are raised all over Spain.

The **Merino sheep** originated in Spain; they are now raised all over the world and provide very good quality wool.

The vineyards of the Douro Valley produce port, a **wine** that is appreciated and sold all over the world.

Rioja, in the northwest of Spain, is an important **wine-producing region**.

Paella, which is rice with meat, fish, and vegetables, is one of the most loved Spanish dishes.

Port was made to last for long journeys. It can age well for up to 80 years.

Most of the Europe's wild **brown bears** live in Asturias, a northern region of Spain.

Manchego, a tasty cheese made with sheep's milk, is named after the La Mancha region where it is made.

Belém (which means "Bethlehem Tower") was built in the 16th century in Lisbon and is a symbol of the capital.

The temperate climate and the great plans of northeast Spain are ideal for growing **crops**.

The Mediterranean coast is home to the main bullfighting arenas, called **plazas de toros**.

Sardines are very popular in Portuguese cooking. They are served **assada** (grilled) and with rice.

The **Pyrenees** are a backdrop to the medieval villages, monasteries, and great forests in the Aragon and Navarre regions.

A Visigoth basilica and a church were built on the site of the **Tarragona Amphitheatre** (2nd century AD).

The Algarve's southern region has interesting **vegetation**, including cacti, agaves, almond trees, and prickly pear trees.

The **toma dei Pirenei** is a delicious cheese from this mountainous and historical region.

The **windmills** of Castilla-La Mancha became famous thanks to the novel *Don Quixote* by Miguel de Cervantes Saavedra.

There are vast beaches with high waves along the northern coast of Portugal, making it perfect for **surfing**.

When creating the **Sagrada Familia Basilica** in Barcelona, Antoni Gaudí played with shape and light to give it a dreamlike atmosphere.

The **Alhambra** is a palace and fortress in Grenada. Its name means "the red one" in Arabic.

Spain

The Galician coasts, in the north of Spain, are full of **shellfish** like the oddly shaped goose barnacles and lobsters.

The **Puerta del Sol** is the central square in Madrid and is the starting point of all Spanish roads.

Fighting bull farms are located mainly in the regions of Andalusia and Extremadura.

Flamenco, the typical Andalusian dance, has over 50 different musical styles, called **palos**.

 Ancient paintings of animals in the **Lascaux cave** were discovered in 1940.

 Normandy **apples** are used to make cider, which goes very well with Camembert cheese.

 Andalusia is also known for Málaga's **grape** production. Grapes from the region are sold all over the world as raisins.

 Bordeaux wine, produced in Aquitaine in France's south-western region, is one the most loved wines in the world.

 The **Chunnel**, or Channel Tunnel, is a famous undersea tunnel that connects the north of France to the south of Great Britain.

 The beaches of Doñana National Park are home to many **sea turtles**.

 Atlantic **oysters** are very popular in Parisian bistros, restaurants, and oyster bars.

 The first big **cycle race** to take place between two cities was the Paris–Rouen in 1869.

 Caravels are small sailing ships that were used by Spanish explorers in the 15th century.

 France's official **sailing school** has about 480 schools across the country.

 A Benedictine monk named Dom Pierre Pérignon helped create the famous sparkling wine called **champagne**.

 The **Balearic Islands** are very popular with tourists and are now one of the richest areas in Spain.

 France has 268 **ports**, including Nantes Saint-Nazaire, Bordeaux, and La Rochelle on the Atlantic coast.

 The **Eiffel Tower** is so famous that there are at least 20 copies of it all over the world.

Principality of Monaco

 The **Monte Carlo Casino** is the most famous building in the city-state of Monaco.

 Ports between Bordeaux and Nantes Saint-Nazaire serve the main international trade routes.

 France is the country with the largest surface area of **pastureland** in the world.

 The **Monaco Grand Prix** is a famous car race around the narrow streets of Monaco.

 The **accordion**, also called "the piano of the poor," is played in many folk music performances in France.

 France has more than 1,200 different types of **cheese**, 50 of which are AOC, which means they are protected trademarks.

France

 The Mediterranean coast of France from Perpignan to Monaco was the birthplace of **seaside tourism**.

 The **Loire Valley** is home to eleven royal castles, or **châteaux**. The most famous among them are Amboise, Chambord, and Chenonceau.

 One of the first French operas, the **Roman de Renart**, has a **fox** as the main character.

 The **Camargue** region is located between the two arms of Europe's largest river delta, the Rhône, and is famous for its horses.

 In the region of Brittany, many **lighthouses** are very tall so that they can be seen above the enormous waves of the Atlantic.

 The Burgundy region produces some of the most famous red and white **wines** in the country.

 One of the most famous French **cheeses**, Roquefort, is produced in the Massif Central region.

 The **Mont Saint Michel Abbey** was founded in the 10th century. It becomes an island when the tide is high.

 The **Tour de France** began in 1903 and is the most famous cycling event in the world.

Founded in 1889, *Michelin* contributed to the creation of the modern-day tire and is also famous for its travel guides.

 A bodice, apron, lace cap, and clogs are all part of *traditional Dutch dress*.

 The *chemical-pharmaceutical industry* is a strong part of the German economy.

 Mont Blanc is the highest peak in the Alps and is almost 15,780 feet (4,810 m) high.

 The Dutch East India Company dominated maritime trade in the 17th and 18th centuries.

 Volkswagen is a famous car company that was founded in Wolfsburg in 1937.

Austria

 High-speed trains, which travel faster than 186 miles per hour (300 kph), run between Italy and France through alpine tunnels.

 Sperm whales, the big whales of the North Sea, can live to up to 70 years old.

 Oktoberfest is a beer festival that is held in the Bavaria region every October.

Luxembourg

 The *Fortress of Luxembourg* was built in the Middle Ages. Its location helped control the land around the Rhine River.

Germany

 Lübeck, Rostock, and Kiel are the major German *ports* for ferries and cruise ships.

 The German Alps are home to many famous *ski resorts*.

Belgium

 A lot of the *coal* mined in the first half of the 20th century came from the Wallonia region of Belgium.

 The *hamburger* was probably invented in the mid-19th century in the city of Hamburg.

 Tyrol is a region in the Alps that is divided in two: the Northern is part is in Austria and the Southern part is in Italy.

 The *Atomium* is a monument dedicated to the atom and to science. It's made of steel and located in Heysel Plateau in Brussels.

 Some German *lighthouses*, like the Roter Sand, a 19th-century monument, are now guesthouses that you can stay in like hotels.

 Austria is a mostly mountainous nation and owes part of its wealth to *alpine tourism*.

 Belgians are known for their comics, including *Tintin*, the most famous comic strip character since 1929.

 Germany is a leading nation in *cattle farming*. The most well-known breeds are the Friesian and the Simmental.

 Sachertorte is a famous Austrian chocolate cake usually served with cream.

The Netherlands

 Beautiful *tulip fields* fill the countryside of the Netherlands in springtime.

 The Brandenburg Gate, the symbol of Berlin since 1791, was inspired by the Propylaea, the entrance to the Acropolis of Athens, Greece.

 Salzburg is known as the European capital of *classical music*. Composer Amadeus Mozart was born in the city.

 The classic *clogs* are made of poplar wood and are part of some of the traditional costumes of the Netherlands.

 The *Rhine-Ruhr metropolitan region* is home to 3,600 people per square mile (1,400 per km²) and is the most densely inhabited metropolitan area in Europe.

 White grapes, like the famous Grüner Veltliner, are grown in eastern Austria.

Switzerland

 Some of the *Dutch windmills*, like those in Kinderdijk, were created to prevent flooding.

 The *wines* of the Rhine region, like Riesling, are celebrated during the traditional wine festival in Rüdesheim am Rhein in August.

 The name of the national capital, Bern, came from the word Bär, which means *"bear"* in German.

Even though the **cuckoo clock** is a typically Swiss product, some believe it was actually designed in the 18th century in the Black Forest in Germany.

Swiss cheese is called Emmental in Switzerland. It's named after the Emmental valley.

The most popular **Swiss cows** are the Simmental and the Brown Swiss breeds.

Italy

The **Mont Blanc massif** is a mountain range with more than 50 peaks.

The Langhe region is known for its Nebbiolo, Barolo, and Barbaresco **wines**.

Turin is considered the Italian capital of the **automobile** industry. The Fiat company creates some of Italy's most famous cars.

The city of Lombardy is considered the birthplace of Italian **industry**.

The Veneto region has a strong **agriculture** industry.

Gondolas are famous boats that are used in the canals of Venice.

The **Ferrari** was first a racing team in 1929. It became a vehicle manufacturer in 1947.

The **Santa Maria del Fiore** is a famous cathedral in Florence. Its dome is one of the largest in the world.

The Italian Riviera is more than 205 miles (330 km) long and is lined with beautiful beaches.

Stamps from the small independent state of San Marino are collectors' items.

The Adriatic Sea is crossed by many **ferries and cruise ships** between Italy, Croatia, and the Greek islands.

Many famous Italian and international films were filmed at Cinecittà, a large **studio** in Rome.

The archaeological site of **Pompeii** was a Roman city that was destroyed by the eruption of Mount Vesuvius in AD 79. It is now an archeological site.

Pizza was invented in Naples and is now sold all over the world. You can even get it in Polynesia and Greenland!

Trulli are houses made of limestone that were built in the region of Puglia starting in the 14th century.

There are 7,000 cone-shaped stone constructions called **nuraghe** that can be found throughout Sardinia. They were probably built by the Nuragic civilization more than 4,000 years ago.

Mount Etna, one of the active volcanoes of the Mediterranean, grew by around 262 feet (80 m) between 1900 and 2010 due to the eruptions.

The Colosseum, which was built in AD 80, is so big that in ancient times real naval battles were held there.

Pecorino Romano is one of the oldest cheeses in the world. It was described in the writings of Pliny the Elder, who was born in AD 23.

Sardinian **beaches** are made up of coral sand, which makes some of them look pink.

Sheep farming was an important part of Sardinian life for centuries.

Pecorino Sardo is a cheese from Sardinia that was created at the end of the 18th century.

The **Etruscan** people lived in parts of Italy from 768 to 264 BC. They brought art like pottery, painting, and sculpture to Italy from Greece.

Oranges were brought to Italy from the Middle East about 1,000 years ago. But the first sweet oranges arrived only at the end of the Middle Ages.

The forests of Sila in the region of Calabria are full of **mushrooms** and home to wolves.

The **Temple of Concordia** is an ancient Greek temple that was built 2,500 years ago in the city of Agrigento in Sicily.

The Monreale Cathedral in Palermo, Sicily, is full of beautiful mosaics made of pure gold.

Malta

The Knights of Malta were forced out of the country in 1798 but are still a symbol of the island nation.

Eastern Europe

RUSSIA

• Moscow

BELARUS

• Minsk

POLAND

• Warsaw

Baltic Sea

Kaliningrad Oblast (RUSSIA)

Lake Onega

Lake Ladoga

VODKA

Kiev

CZECH REPUBLIC

Prague

SLOVAKIA

Bratislava

HUNGARY

Budapest

UKRAINE

MOLDOVA

Chișinău

ROMANIA

Bucharest

SLOVENIA

Ljubljana

CROATIA

Zagreb

Belgrade

SERBIA

BOSNIA AND
HERZEGOVINA Sarajevo

MONTENEGRO

Podgorica

KOSOVO

Pristina

MACEDONIA

Skopje

BULGARIA

Sofia

Black Sea

TURKEY

ALBANIA

Tirana

GREECE

Athens

Mykonos

Rhodes

Aegean Sea

Crete

CYPRUS

Mediterranean Sea

Link to download the map:

https://www.hachettebookgroup.com/eastern-europe

Eastern Europe

Slovenia

 The **Dragon Bridge**, built in 1901 in Ljubljana, was dedicated to the emperor Franz Joseph I of Austria.

 Half of Slovenia is covered in mountains, so **alpine sports** are very important for tourism.

 Lipica was the birthplace of Lipizzaner **horses**.

Croatia

 The **Art Pavilion** in Zagreb is the oldest gallery in southeastern Europe.

 The **Pula Arena** hosted combats between gladiators and small ships in the 1st century AD.

 The regions of Istria and Dalmatia have hundreds of miles of **swimming beaches** and more than 1,200 islands.

 Ćevapčići are balls of meat sold as **street food** all over Croatia.

Serbia

 The **Church of Saint Sava** in Belgrade is one of the largest Orthodox churches in the world.

 Đerdap National Park, which is next to the Danube River, is home to the **lynx**.

 Zastava cars were produced in the city of Kragujevac until 2008.

 Serbia is world-renowned for its **basketball** team.

Kosovo

 The **Fatih Mosque**, also known as the Imperial Mosque, is the main mosque in Pristina and is located in the center of the Old Town.

Montenegro

 The **Millennium Bridge** in Podgorica connects the riverbanks of the Morača River.

 The **Ostrog Monastery** was founded in the 17th century in a cliff face 2,950 feet (900 m) from the ground.

Bosnia and Herzegovina

 At 574 feet (175 m) high, the **Avaz Twist Tower** in Sarajevo is the highest skyscraper in all of the Balkans.

 The traditional **Bosnian costume** is still worn to dance the **kolo**, a traditional collective dance.

 The **Stari Most** in Mostar was a 16th-century Ottoman bridge destroyed by war in 1993 and rebuilt in 2004.

Macedonia

 The **Museum of Macedonia** was built in 1924.

 Archeologists believe that the Slavic alphabet was created by two monks at the **Church of Saints Clement and Panteleimon**.

Albania

 There is a statue dedicated to the national hero **Skanderbeg**, who was a military commander in the Ottoman empire, in the capital city of Tirana.

 During the Gjirokastër National Folklore Festival, people dress up in **traditional Albanian costumes**.

 The magnificent **beaches** on the Adriatic and Ionian coasts are big tourist attractions.

 Djathë (pecorino), **filicat** (giuncata), and **gjize** (ricotta) are Albania's most popular cheeses.

Greece

 The **Parthenon** is a temple in Athens, Greece, that was built in the 5th century BC. It housed a giant statue of the goddess Athena made of more than 2,200 pounds (1,000 kg) of gold.

 Wars were suspended in ancient times when the **Olympic games** were played.

 Syrtos is a famous ancient Greek folk dance that is still performed on some islands.

 Mount Athos is called "Holy Mountain" in Greek and is home to 20 different monasteries and more than 2,000 people.

According to mythology, **Mount Olympus** is the home of the 12 main gods of the ancient Greek world.

Millions of people visit the archaeological sites and the **beaches** of the island of Crete every year.

The character of **Dracula** was inspired by a real person, Prince Vlad III of Romania. He was called "Son of the Dragon" (**dracul** in Romanian).

Hoplites were foot soldiers in ancient Greece. They wore heavy shields and feathered helmets.

Bulgaria

The **Saint Alexander Nevsky Cathedral** in Sofia is home to some of the most important art in the country.

The **pelican** is the symbol of the Danube River, which is Europe's second-longest river.

Prickly pears are grown nearly everywhere in Greece and throughout other Mediterranean countries.

One Bulgarian out of four still works in the fields, growing **grain** and sunflowers.

Barbastels are bats that live in the Carpathian Mountains. They are small in size, and live in enormous groups.

Moldova

Amphorae were the most common container used to hold liquid or grains in ancient times.

Bulgaria is considered the country of the **rose**.

Stephen III, or **Stephen the Great**, is considered the father of the Moldova. He is also a saint.

The ships of the **Merchant Marine of Greece** can carry more cargo than any other navy in the world.

Traditional Bulgarian costumes are hand-sewn and are reminiscent of Balkan and Asian dress.

Grapes have been grown in Moldova for 5,000 years.

Hungary

The Greek islands are a **sailing** paradise, thanks to the beauty of the sea that surrounds them and the constant wind.

Windsurfing is very popular on the Bulgarian Black Sea coast.

The **Hungarian Parliament Building** was completed in 1904 and is the largest building in Hungary, with 691 rooms.

Romania

Dolphins are symbols of beauty and believed to be good omens, and are often a part of Greek stories.

The **Palace of the Parliament** is considered the heaviest and the second-widest building in the world.

Fencing is a very popular sport in Hungary.

The Mycenaean people used the writing system called **Linear B** between the 15th and 13th centuries BC. They wrote down their language on clay tablets.

Oină, which has similar rules to baseball, was invented in the 14th century in Wallachia and is still played today.

The Puszta is a large prairieland between the Danube and Tisza rivers. It is home to famous horse stables where shows are performed.

The island of Mykonos is known for its **windmills**.

The **Easter tradition of painting eggs** has become an art form in the Bukovina region.

The Bear Park in Veresegyház, Budapest, is a small farm and zoo home to about 40 bears that live in wide spaces with hills and trees.

The **Minotaur** was a monster in Greek mythology that lived in a labyrinth, or maze, on the island of Crete.

The **Merry Cemetery** in Săpânţa is known for its bright colors, votive paintings, and floral decorations.

About 20 percent of Hungarian territory is covered in forests full of **deer**, bears, and wolves.

Franz Liszt is one of the great classical composers of the 19th century and also one of the most famous Hungarians in the world.

 The **fujara** is a big flute used in Slovakian folk music that can be up to 6 feet (2 m) long.

 According to the legend, spooky **witches' sabbaths** were once held on Łysa Góra (Bald Mountain).

 Tokaji, or Tokay, is a Hungarian wine that was once given as a precious gift between nobles and clerics.

Poland

 The Mermaid of Warsaw statue is a symbol of a romantic Polish legend. Some people believe it protects the city of Warsaw.

 The Polish plains produce more than 28 million tons (25 million metric tons) of **grain** every year.

Czech Republic

 The Nationale-Nederlanden in Prague is nicknamed the **Dancing House** because the building looks a little like a pair of dancers.

 The rare żubr **bison** is the biggest and oldest European land animal and lives in the forests of Poland.

Belarus

 The **National Library of Belarus** in Minsk is located inside a building that looks a bit like a spaceship.

 April 30 is known as **Čarodejnice**, or witch burning night, in the Czech Republic. In this ancient tradition, the Czechs burn a fake witch to symbolize the end of winter.

 The **Knights Templar** built medieval fortresses in Poland like the one in Marienburg, which is one of the most popular tourist destinations in Europe.

 Minsk was the capital of the **punk** scene in Europe until the end of the 1980s.

 Pilsner Urquell is a Czech beer brewed in the city of Plzeň.

 Gray seals are protected in the Mewia Łacha Nature Reserve on the Baltic Sea.

 Beavers have almost disappeared from many parts of Europe where they used to live, but they can still be found in the Dnieper River basin.

 Ice hockey is one of the most popular sports in the Czech Republic.

 There is a **stork** village in Pentowo that is home to more than 100 storks. The Poles believe that the **birds** bring good luck.

 Every year in Belarus, more than 30 **folk festivals** take place that are inspired by rural traditions.

 There are many **windmills** between the cities Kuželov and Bílovec that still work today.

 The great **pianist** Frédéric Chopin was born in Żelazowa Wola, near Warsaw.

 Belarus is made up of extensive plains that are perfect for **road bicycle racing**.

Slovakia

 The **Bratislava Castle** was built in the 10th century and is on the 10-, 20-, and 50-cent Euro coins.

 The Main Square in **Kraków Old Town** is the biggest medieval plaza in Europe.

 The **Cherry Festival** is held every year in the town of Glubokoe.

Ukraine

 The **High Tatras** is a mountain range in northern Slovakia that is a popular Slovakian ski destination.

 The city of Zakopane is on the Polish side of the Tatra Mountains and is a popular **skiing** destination.

 The **Kiev Pechersk Lavra** is a monastery in the city of Kiev that is considered the spiritual center of the Ukrainian Orthodox Church.

Dnipro was home to a **nuclear arms** factory and the space industry when Ukraine was part of the Soviet Union.

 The **Winter Palace** in St. Petersburg was the winter home of the family of the Tsar of Russia.

 The most well-known **traditional Russian item of clothing** is the **sarafan**, a traditional folk costume worn by Russian women and girls.

 The **Cossacks** were a group of people who lived in the south of the Ukraine that were known for being proud and brave fighters.

 The **Trans-Siberian Railway** is the longest railway in the world and passes through eight time zones.

 Northern Russia is snowy for six months of the year and has produced many cross-country **skiing** champions.

 Kharkiv was home to the KhPZ factory that famously made a very large **tractor** called the Kharkovchanka.

 Sergiyev Posad is known for the **Trinity Lavra of St. Sergius**, the most important monastery in Russia.

 The **Novgorod Kremlin** was built in 1044 and is Russia's oldest fortress.

 The vyshyvanka, the **traditional Ukranian dress**, has embroidery that requires months of work.

 In Russia's arctic regions, **reindeer** farming is the only means of livelihood.

 The Russian astronaut Yuri Gagarin was the first man in **space**.

 Built between 1911 and 1912 on a cliff overlooking the sea, the **Swallow's Nest** is a beautiful castle near the city of Yalta.

 There are about 200,000 **brown bears** in the world. They live in Russia, China, and North America.

 The Bolshoi Ballet is one of the oldest and most famous **ballet** companies in the world.

 The ancient city of **Chersonesus** was built by the Greeks about 2,500 years ago. Its ruins are a tourist attraction today.

 The famous Russian-Ukrainian **dance** called **kozachok** is part of the culture of the Cossack people.

European Turkey

 The **Blue Mosque** in Istanbul is covered with more than 20,000 handmade tiles.

European Russia

 Saint Basil's Cathedral is decorated with beautiful colors and is one of the most famous buildings in Moscow.

 Many Russians wear **fur coats** during the very cold Russian winters.

 Turkey exports more **sunflower** oil than any other country.

Cyprus

 Soviet nuclear **submarines** were the largest submarines ever built.

 The **sleigh** Russians use for traveling is called a *troika* ("triple") because it is pulled by three horses.

 The **Phoenician juniper** (*Juniperus phoenicea*) tree is a symbol of the island country of Cyprus.

RUSSIA

KAZAKHSTAN

MONGOLIA

Black Sea

Caspian Sea

GEORGIA
ARMENIA
AZERBAIJAN

UZBEKISTAN

KYRGYZSTAN

TURKMENISTAN

TAJIKISTAN

CHINA

TURKEY

NORTHERN
CYPRUS

LEBANON

SYRIA

IRAQ

IRAN

AFGHANISTAN

STATE OF
PALESTINE

ISRAEL

JORDAN

KUWAIT

Sinai
(EGYPT)

SAUDI
ARABIA

BAHRAIN
QATAR

UNITED
ARAB EMIRATES

PAKISTAN

NEPAL

BHUTAN

INDIA

BANGLADESH

MYANMAR

VIET

LAOS

Red Sea

OMAN

YEMEN

Arabian
Sea

Bay
of Bengal

THAILAND

CAMB

SRI LANKA

ANDAMAN AND
NICOBAR ISLANDS
(INDIA)

MA

MALDIVES

Kara Sea

Indian Ocean

Laptev Sea

East Siberian Sea

Chukchi Sea

Bering Sea

Sea of Okhotsk

NORTH KOREA

SOUTH KOREA

Sea of Japan

JAPAN

Yellow Sea

East China Sea

TAIWAN

South China Sea

PHILIPPINES

BRUNEI

Celebes Sea

SIA

INDONESIA

Asia

Pacific Ocean

Population:
4.5 billion

Surface area:
**17.2 million square miles
(44 milion km²)**

Link to download the map:

https://www.hachettebookgroup.com/asia

43

Asia
The Endless Continent

The Asia of today looks huge, but it's really a puzzle made up of lots of pieces called tectonic plates. These plates are underneath all the land and water on Earth and constantly move—but very slowly. As they shifted billions of years ago in different places across the surface of the Earth, they moved closer to each other until they stuck together.

Asia is a young and active continent. Its mountains continue to grow, and earthquakes happen often. It also has many volcanoes, like Krakatoa in Indonesia, which erupted in 1883; the beautiful Mount Fuji in Japan, which has been dormant since 1707; and the volcano chain on the Kamchatka Peninsula in northeast Russia.

Asia's thick crust contains coal reserves, gas and oil deposits, and rare metals that are necessary to modern technology. Also, Asia's coastlines, one and a half times longer than the Earth's circumference, provide lots of maritime resources.

Asia is crossed by a ridge of mountain ranges that runs from Europe to Malaysia. This means that the continent forms a sort of "roof" that collects enormous quantities of rainfall on the southern slope.

That rainfall created big rivers like the Yellow River in China and the Yenisei and Ob Rivers in Siberia. There are exceptional lakes like Lake Baikal in Russia, the deepest (5,315 feet/1,620 m) and oldest lake in the world.

Asia has both of the highest mountains in the world: Mount Everest in Nepal (29,035 feet/8,850 m) and K2 in Pakistan and China (28,251 feet/8,611 m). It also has some of the lowest points on Earth. The Challenger Deep on the floor of the Pacific Ocean is 36,200 feet (11,034 m) deep, the surface of the Dead Sea in the Middle East is 1,410 feet (430 m) below sea level, and the Krubera Cave in Georgia, the deepest cave on Earth, is 7,208 feet (2,197 m) deep.

Asia is home to both the coldest place on Earth, in Siberia (-94°F/-70°C), and one of the hottest, in Iran (129°F/54°C). The big climate differences create deserts like the Gobi desert, but also stretches of green vegetation like forests, jungle, large grass plains, and savannas (grasslands).

Each climate has its own inhabitants. Asia is home to legendary animals like snow leopards and elephants. The last wild tigers in the world live in the forests between China and Russia. More than one-third of the planet's forests are located in Asia.

Asia is also the origin of many types of crops, including wheat, which was grown for the first time 11,000 years ago in what is now Turkey; and rice, the main staple food in Asia, which was first planted in China and India more than 13,000 years ago.

Asia is between Africa, Europe, and America. *Homo erectus*, an early relative of humans, came to Asia from Africa about 2 million years ago. Once they arrived in the huge Eurasia, they explored the whole continent, arriving in China 1.7 million years ago.

A long time later *Homo sapiens* arrived, reaching Australia 40,000 years ago, Siberia 30,000 years ago, and finally, the Pacific Islands 3,300 years ago.

Humans created great things all over Asia. One was the Silk Road, an ancient trade route between China and Europe. Thriving cities like Xi'an in China and Samarkand in Uzbekistan grew along the route.

Asia has witnessed the emergence and disappearance of entire human civilizations since it was first inhabited millions of years ago.

Asian populations have a variety of different customs and have followed them for a very long time.

Sumerians, who lived in modern-day Iraq 4,000 years ago, may have shared some features of their writing system with the civilizations of the Indus Valley in modern-day Pakistan and India.

Asia is home to more than half of the human race. There are millions of people living in the urban areas of China and India, but in large territories like Siberia in Russia there are very few people or even animals.

The biggest cities in the world are in Asia. Shanghai in China has 24 million people, and Istanbul in Turkey has 15 million people. The oldest cities are there, too, like Jericho in the territory of Palestine, which is 11,000 years old, and Byblos in Lebanon, which was founded at least 9,000 years ago.

There are many different industries active in Asia today. Industrial basins and mining sites, nuclear power stations, and some of the biggest seaports in the world are spread across this one continent.

Asia's majestic nature has inspired many legends. It is said that the Arabian deserts are inhabited by the jinn (genies), that the Himalayas are the last dwelling place of the Yeti (the Abominable Snowman), and that China is the land of dragons. The Garden of Eden can supposedly be found somewhere between Iraq, Azerbaijan, and Armenia.

Kara Sea

RUSSIA

KAZAKHSTAN

Qstana

MONGOLIA

Ulaanbaatar

Laptev
Sea

East Siberian
Sea

Chukchi
Sea

Bering
Sea

Sea of
Okhotsk

Northern Asia and Kazakhstan

Northern Asia and Kazakhstan

Asian Russia

 The **Siberian** people wear warm and colorful fur clothes, similar to those worn by the European Sami people who live in Norway, Sweden, and Finland.

 The remote, rushing rivers of this area are popular destinations for extreme **kayaking**.

 Different kinds of **brown bears** live in the great deserted spaces of Russia.

 Ice hockey is a well-loved sport in Russia, whose national team is among the best in the world.

 The fur hat called the **ushanka** is essential in some areas of Russia where temperatures can fall below -58°F (-50°C).

 In Russia, tea is traditionally made using a **samovar**, a kettle-like container with a faucet.

 Important **automotive** manufacturers like LADA and Ural, which produces motorcycles, are located in the region of the Ural Mountains.

 Matryoshka dolls, which are placed one inside the other, are painted wearing the costumes of the different regions of Russia.

 In the heart of Russia, **skis** are still used by those who need to cross the snow on foot, just as they were thousands of years ago.

 A tall fur hat is part of the costume worn by the **Cossacks**, a people known for their pride and independence.

 The **Novosibirsk railway station** is a big bright-green building and is an important stop along the Trans-Siberian Railway.

 Sturgeon roe are the eggs of a fish that live both in rivers and the sea. They are used to make delicious **caviar**.

 The **balalaika**, like a triangular guitar with three strings, accompanies music and dance all over Russia.

 People like the **Dolgans** live in northern Russia. Their way of life is similar to that of the Inuit people in North America.

 Some areas of northern Russia are so isolated that they can only be traveled to by **ski-plane**.

 The **reindeer** is a type of deer that lives in the arctic and subarctic regions.

 The **musk ox** is a kind of ox that lived in Russia during the time of the mammoths, but then disappeared from the area. Today they have been reintroduced in small groups in Siberia.

 Horse-pulled sleighs are still used as a mode of transportation in Russia.

People in northern Russia take *ice baths* when they are kids to get their bodies used to the cold.

 Long freight trains and passengers have been using the *Trans-Siberian Railway*, which is over 5,600 miles (9,000 km) long, for more than 100 years.

 Siberian salmon, called *taimen*, live in rivers like the Amur River. They feed on fish, lizards, and rodents.

 Vodka is made from grains and potatoes and is the Russian national drink.

 Big *nuclear submarines* sail beneath the frozen waters of northern Russia. Some of them are as long as two football fields.

 The *Siberian tiger* has a lighter-colored coat than its Indian relative and is sometimes almost white, with black stripes.

 Tents used by Siberian herders are called *chums*. They are very similar to the tepees of the Native Americans.

 The Siberian nomadic *reindeer* herders learn from a young age how to use a lasso to keep the herd together.

 The Russian aircraft *Antonov An-225* was first built in 1985 and is the heaviest aircraft ever built.

 An explosion that killed 80 million trees near the *Tunguska River* in 1908 was caused by a small meteoroid.

 Siberia is partly covered by the *taiga*, which is a forest full of firs and pines that provides large amounts of timber.

 Sakhalin Oblast has large *gas and oil* reserves that are important for the Russian economy.

 The *snow leopard* still lives in the most isolated areas of Russia and high in the mountains, but is becoming more and more rare.

 Thousands of miles of *pipeline* carry precious oil and gas to the east, toward Europe.

 The *polar bear* lives in the Arctic in Canada, Norway, Alaska, and Russia.

 Siberia is home to some of the richest *diamond deposits* in the world.

 The *Vostochny Cosmodrome* is a spaceport in eastern Russia. It launched its first spacecraft on April 28, 2016.

 Ringed seals get their name from their coats, which have dark markings encircled by light gray rings.

 The *Mir mine* is an abandoned diamond mine in Siberia. It's 1,722 feet (525 m) deep and is one of the largest open pits in the world.

 A monument shaped like mammoth tusks stands in the *Pole of Cold* in Verkhoyansk, which is one of the coldest cities in the world.

 The big *icebreaker ships* are the only ships able to sail the seas of northern Russia in every season.

Falconry has been practiced in central Asia for many centuries. In Kazakhstan, the best falconers use eagles.

The **dombra** is an instrument of Mongolian origin and is one of the symbols of Kazakhstan.

Dogsleds have been used in the arctic regions for at least 3,000 years.

A **woolly mammoth calf** was found preserved near Magadan. The long-haired animal became extinct at the end of the ice age.

The **Kazakh horse** is small, but it is lively and energetic.

Kazakhstan is rich in uranium, chromium, diamonds, and **gold**. They have some of biggest deposits of these resources in the world.

In Yakut legends, the **Snow Maiden** wears elaborate clothing inspired by the traditional garments of this freezing-cold region.

The **calpac** is a pointed hat worn throughout Kazakhstan.

The **opium poppy** that grows in central Asia used to be used to relieve pain during ancient times, both in Egypt and in Rome.

The **fur ushanka hat**, the traditional headgear in this area, is also worn as an elegant accessory for women.

The first man in space, the **cosmonaut** Yuri Gagarin, was launched from the Baikonur Cosmodrome in 1961.

The **Tian Shan** mountain range, or the Mountains of Heaven, begins in East Kazakhstan with icy peaks up to 22,966 feet (7,000 m) high.

Walruses live in the Arctic Ocean and have tusks that weigh up to 12 pounds (5.4 kg).

The **Kazakhstan Central Concert Hall** in the capital city of Astana is shaped like a flower.

Koumiss is a mildly alcoholic traditional Asian drink made from sweet horse's milk.

There are 29 **active volcanoes** on the Kamchatka Peninsula.

Kazakhstan exports large quantities of **grain** abroad. The people of Kazakhstan have been farming for centuries.

The **saker falcon** chases its prey by flying next to it rather than attacking from above like other falcons.

The **red king crab** has a leg span of up to 6 feet (1.8 m).

Armor made of felt (a thick wool fabric), leather, and fur was worn by warriors in central Asia during the Bronze Age, about 4,000 years ago.

The **Przewalski's horse** is the last truly wild horse in the world.

Mongolia

 The **Mongolian pheasant** lives in the country's few woodland areas and is larger than the common pheasant.

 There is a statue of **Genghis Khan** near the capital city of Ulaanbaatar. Khan founded the biggest empire in history 800 years ago.

 The trains on the **Trans-Mongolian Railway** cross the country for 690 miles (1,110 km) and pass through the Gobi desert.

 The **morin khuur**, similar to a violin, is the traditional Mongolian instrument.

 The **Bactrian camel** has two humps and lives in the wild in the Gobi desert.

 The giant **dump trucks** used in the mines of Mongolia can carry up to 400 tons (362 metric tons) of coal. That's the equivalent of what 20 regular trucks could hold all together.

 **Wrestling** is Mongolia's national sport. Athletes wear an outfit that leaves the chest and legs uncovered.

 The white Buddhist monuments called **stupas** are scattered across the vast Mongolian landscapes, where Tibetan Buddhism is the most popular religion.

 The tents of Mongolian herders are called **yurts**. They are made of wood and felt and can be put up and removed easily.

Central Asia, the Near East, and India

Link to download the map:

https://www.hachettebookgroup.com/central-asia

UZBEKISTAN

Tashkent

Bishkek

KYRGYZSTAN

Dushanbe

TAJIKISTAN

Kabul

AFGHANISTAN

Islamabad

PAKISTAN

New Delhi

NEPAL

Kathmandu

Thimphu

BHUTAN

BANGLADESH

Dhaka

INDIA

Arabian
Sea

Bay
of
Bengal

Indian Ocean

MALDIVES

Malé

SRI LANKA

Colombo

Andaman and
Nicobar Islands

Central Asia, the Near East, and India

Turkey (Asia)

 This customary bronze symbol represents the **Sun Disc** of the Hittites, an Indo-European people who lived 3,500 years ago in what is now Turkey.

 Troy, the city conquered by the Achaeans about 3,200 years ago thanks to the trick of the **Trojan horse**, is located in Turkey near the modern-day city of Çanakkale.

 The two-story facade of the **Library of Celsus** (2nd century AD) is one of the most fascinating ruins of the splendid Ephesus, an ancient city that was called Apasa during the Trojan War era.

 The hot springs of **Pamukkale**, whose water is rich in calcium, have created a landscape of natural white walkways found nowhere else in the world.

 The **tombs** excavated 2,300 years ago from the rock overlooking the Dalyan Çayi River are perfect reproductions of the facades of temples that existed during the time of Alexander the Great (4th century BC).

 Nasreddin Hodja, a fictional character famous across the whole of western Asia, rides a donkey facing backward so he never turns his back on the people following him.

 Turkey's ancient volcanoes are extinct, but left marvels such as the hardened lava rock formations of the town of **Göreme**, once used as dwellings and monasteries.

 Sufi whirling is a dance practiced by a religious order, in which the dancer spins around repeatedly to become closer to God.

 The great heads of Zeus, Apollo, and other gods atop **Mount Nemrut** were sculpted on the orders of Antiochus I Theos of Commagene, king of the Kingdom of Commagene, a faithful ally of Rome.

 In northeast Turkey, the mountains that extend up toward the Caucasus Mountains are often covered in snow and are home to several **ski resorts**.

 Some Christians believe **Noah's Ark** landed on Mount Ararat.

Cyprus

 Aphrodite is the Greek goddess of beauty and love. According to myth, she was born from the waters of Cyprus.

Syria

 A **scimitar** is a sword with a curved blade from the Middle East.

 The cone shape of the **beehive houses** of Syria help to cool down the indoor temperature. The heat rises like in a chimney and exits the house through a hole in the top of the dome.

 The **Syrian hamster** is very active. It runs for several hours each day in search of food and cleans its burrow to perfection.

 The **date palm** produces a sweet fruit, and its shade allows other plants, like the fig tree, to grow in the Syrian heat.

Lebanon

 The **cedars of Lebanon** are giant, beautiful trees that once filled big forests. The Ancient Egyptians purchased large quantities of these trees.

Israel

 The Western Wall, also known as the **Wailing Wall**, and the **Al-Aqsa Mosque** (Temple Mount) in Jerusalem stand on the site where the Second Temple was built. It was destroyed in AD 70.

Jordan

 The ancient city of **Petra** is in the Jordan desert. Its monumental tombs in the shape of temples were cut out of the rock about 2,000 years ago.

 The **Androctonus** or fattail scorpion is very poisonous. Its name means "man-killer."

Saudia Arabia

 Kingdom Centre is a 992-foot (302-m) skyscraper in the capital city of Riyadh that is lit up by multicolored lights at night.

 Oil, Saudi Arabia's most precious resource, was discovered in 1938 after a long search.

 Gerbils that live in the desert camouflage themselves well, thanks to their sand-colored fur.

 The **fennec fox** is a small fox with very long, oversized ears that can hear each and every noise (like the slithering of a snake).

Inside the Great Mosque of Mecca is the *Kaaba,* a sacred building that represents the heart of the Islamic religion and contains the Black Stone, possibly a fragment of a meteorite.

Stone, wood, straw, and clay are the materials used to build the *traditional houses* in southern Saudi Arabia, which are always equipped with a well or are near a watering hole.

The *kaffiyeh* is a cotton scarf in two colors that men wrap around their heads. It is the traditional headgear of the Middle East.

Limousines as long as buses are the cars used by sheikhs, who are leaders in the Arab world.

Bedouin tents are still used in the deserts of Saudi Arabia.

The *camel* is the best transport method in the Arabian deserts. Their slim legs and toed hooves spread out on the sand.

Yemen

Dar al-Hajar is a spectacular palace that was built on a rock outside the capital city of Sana'a.

Oman

The dome of the *Al Lawati Mosque* in Muscat, the capital of Oman, is covered in magnificent mosaics in shades of turquoise and blue.

Nakhal Fort was built on rock and completed in 1834 to protect trade routes. Today it's a mosque and a museum.

Arabian camels usually walk slowly, but sometimes they are raced in thrilling contests.

The *jinn,* or *genies*, are supernatural beings of ancient origin that can be good or bad, just like human beings.

United Arab Emirates

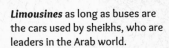
The modern *Sheikh Zayed Mosque* in Abu Dhabi is full of decorations made with precious materials and created by artisans from many parts of the world.

The *Burj Khalifa* in Dubai is the tallest building ever built by man. It is 2,720 feet (829 m) tall, which is almost twice as high as the Empire State Building in New York.

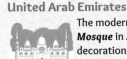
Dhows are traditional sailing boats in the Persian Gulf. They have a large triangular sail and were used to trade products with India in ancient times.

Qatar

Qatar hosts a *Formula 1 Powerboat Grand Prix* race.

Bahrain

The *Bahrain Grand Prix* is a car race held once a year in Bahrain.

Kuwait

The *Kuwait Towers* are three towers with three spheres in the capital city of Kuwait City. Two of the spheres are water tanks and the third holds a restaurant.

Iran

According to some, the spiral shape of the *minaret at the Great Mosque of Samarra*, which was built more than 1,000 years ago, was inspired by those of the ancient Babylonian temples.

The *Ishtar Gate* is completely covered in blue tiles, and was made using bricks from the walls of the ancient city of Babylon.

The *magic carpet* appears in Middle Eastern and Russian folklore. In some stories it can transport itself instantly to anywhere in the world, and in others it flies on the wings of the wind instead.

Georgia

The modern *Holy Trinity Cathedral* of Tbilisi, the capital of Georgia, is one of the biggest churches in the world. The cross on its dome is 287 feet (87 m) from the ground.

Armenia

The colorful *traditional garments* of Armenia were first made 3,000 years ago using wool, cotton, and silk trimmed with fur.

Azerbaijan

In Baku, the capital of Azerbaijan, there are unusual skyscrapers like the *Flame Towers*, which is a trio of towers that look like big flames.

The famous *carpets* of Azerbaijan are still made by hand. The beginning and the end of the work are celebrated with big parties.

Iraq

The *Azadi Tower* in the capital city of Tehran was completed in 1971 to commemorate the 2,500th year of the foundation of Cyrus the Great's empire.

Beluga caviar, the most expensive in the world, comes from the Caspian Sea in northern Iran.

Polo is a modern version of the game played by the ancient Persians that exists across central Asia.

Modern *power plants* produce energy thanks to the rich gas and oil resources that make Iran an energy superpower.

Arabian leopards are half the size of African and Asian leopards and have a lighter-colored coat.

The *veiled chameleon* lives in Yemen and Oman.

Pelicans spend the winter in the heat of Iran after having spent the summer in the cool climate of Russia.

Turkmenistan

 Heroes and other famous people from Turkmenistan are shown as statues at the bottom of the **Independence Monument** in the capital city of Ashgabat.

 Uzbek orchestras include the **kernei,** a brass trumpet 6.5 feet (2 m) long that is usually only played outside, as it produces a very loud sound.

 Decorated with magnificent mosaics made of colored tiles, the **Shah Mosque** in Isfahan was built about 400 years ago and is one of the most beautiful mosques in the Islamic world.

 The traditional Turkmen **tent** is a type of yurt decorated on the outside with strips of fabric called **kapunuk**.

Kyrgyzstan

 Kyrgyz **ballad singers** tell the adventures of the national hero Manas by reciting a poem that is 40 times longer than the *Odyssey*.

 Chess may have been invented in India, but the game's name comes from Persia, where it's called **shah**, which means "[game of the] king."

 **Camels** are still used as transportation in Turkmenistan.

 The steppes of central Asia 2,800 years ago belonged to the **Scyths**, who were horsemen and goldsmiths.

Tajikistan

 Karakul sheep have been raised for centuries for their milk, wool, fur, and meat. They are capable of surviving in dry climates thanks to the fat that accumulates in their tails.

 Turkmen garments are made in many colors, but red is the most common color worn by both men and women.

 In the capital of Tajikistan, Dushanbe, an intricately decorated arch honors **Rudaki**, the first great Persian poet, who lived 1,100 years ago.

Afghanistan

 Even though it's usually associated with Holland, the **tulip** is a flower of eastern origin, and some varieties come from Afghanistan.

 The **Great Kyz Kala** was a fortified palace built around 1,000 years ago. Its ruins can be seen today in the city of Sultan Kala.

Pakistan

 Obi non is a traditional bread from Tajikistan and other countries in Central Asia. It is round, flat in the middle, and thicker and decorated around the edges.

 The **Afghan hound** is proud and independent. It has been bred for centuries in Afghanistan where it's used for hunting.

 The **Door to Hell** is a crater in the heart of Turkmenistan that has been burning since 1971, when it was set on fire to avoid an environmental disaster after a drilling operation went wrong.

 The shape of the **Faisal Mosque** in Islamabad is similar to a Bedouin tent and without the traditional dome. The mosque is an example of modern Islamic architecture.

 The blue **lapis lazuli** is a precious stone that can be found in Afghanistan.

Uzbekistan

 The **Khast-Imam Complex** in the capital city of Tashkent was built 500 years ago with a great entrance that makes the other buildings look tiny.

 The **Indus river dolphin** only lives in the Indus River and is almost blind.

 The **markhor** is a wild goat that lives in the mountains of Afghanistan. Its name, meaning "serpent," comes from its long, twisted horns.

 In the city of Bukhara, four impressive towers surround the **Charminar**, a **madrassa** (religious school) with rooms for the students, a water cistern, and a mosque.

 Field hockey comes from sports played for centuries in central Asia. Pakistan's national team is one of the best in the world.

 It is thought that the pomegranate was first grown in Afghanistan, where it is still an important product.

 The **Bactrian camel** can go months without water and can walk for 24 hours in a row. When it fills up on water, it drinks more than 26 gallons (100 L)!

The walls of the ancient **Derawar Fort** are as tall as a 10-story palace and almost 12,000 years old.

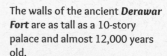

The Karakoram is a mountain range in northern Pakistan that is home to **K2**, 28,245 feet (8,609 m), the second-highest peak in the world.

According to a legend, the smiling faces of **Jagannath** (a form of the god Krishna) and his brothers are so strange because their original statues were left incomplete.

The Sri Lankan **Oruwa canoe** is a double-hull canoe with a square sail.

India

The **Taj Mahal** in Agra was built 400 years ago using expensive materials and precious decorations. It looks like a fairy-tale palace.

The adventures of **Mowgli** and the ferocious **Shere Khan** told in **The Jungle Book** are set in the forests of Seoni in the northeast of the country, where today there is a tiger reserve.

Nepal

In Nepal, some little girls are believed to have the spirit of the goddess **Kumari** inside of them.

The **Golden Temple** in Amritsar is the most holy site for the religion of Sikhism, which is practiced is northern India.

In India, the **cow** is sacred and worshipped. It must not be killed.

Mount Everest is the highest mountain in the world and straddles the border between Nepal and China (Tibet).

The **elephant** is a sacred animal in India, but it was also used in the past during wars and to carry things like lumber.

Curry is the typical Indian food, made with many spices that give it a variety of flavors, from mild to spicy.

Legend has it that the **Yeti**, or Abominable Snowman, lives in the mountains of the Himalayas.

The technological revolution is transforming India, where the number of **smartphones** and other devices is increasing day by day.

Tea picking is done mostly by women in the northeast of the country, where the climate is very rainy and perfect for growing tea.

Bhutan

Archery is Bhutan's national sport and is practiced by men and women, who wear traditional costumes during competitions.

More than just a tradition, the **sari** is the most common piece of clothing worn by millions of Indian women. They are of silk, cotton, or artificial fibers and are always very colorful.

On the outer edge of northeast India, along the India-Myanmar border, live the **Naga** people, who were once feared headhunters and who still practice many of their cultural traditions today.

Bangladesh

The **Nymphaea stellata** is a sacred plant that is also used as a medicine. It's the national flower of Bangladesh, and it lives in still pond water.

Ganesha is an Indian god with an elephant's head that helps humans who are struggling with the difficulties of life. He's the main character in many myths and legends.

Maldives

A typical inhabitant of the coral reefs is the **clown fish**.

The **rickshaw** is the most commonly used "taxi" in Bangladesh and is decorated with bright-colored pictures.

Yoga was born in India thousands of years ago and is now popular all over the world. It's a practice that uses meditation, breathing techniques, and exercise.

Sri Lanka

In Sri Lanka, some fishermen stand on stilts in the ocean instead of boats.

Indian **snake charmers** learn how to protect themselves against snake venom when they are children.

The **peacock** comes from southern Asia and is very common in Sri Lanka.

CHINA

MYANMAR

Nay Pyi Taw

VIETNAM

Hanoi

LAOS

Vientiane

THAILAND

Bangkok

Phnom Penh

CAMBODIA

Eastern Asia

Bay
of
Bengal

NORTH KOREA

Pyongyang

Seoul

SOUTH KOREA

Yellow
Sea

Beijing

East China Sea

Sea of Japan

JAPAN

Tokyo

Pacific Ocean

Taipei

TAIWAN

South
China
Sea

Manila

PHILIPPINES

Kuala Lumpur

MALAYSIA

SINGAPORE

Singapore

INDONESIA

Jakarta

Celebes
Sea

BRUNEI

Bandar
Seri Begawan

EAST TIMOR

Dili

59

Eastern Asia

China

Falconry, a widespread practice among the nomadic people of the northwest, is mentioned in Chinese documents from 2,700 years ago. Today, it is mostly practiced as a sport.

Dumplings are made all over China. In the region of Xinjiang they are called **chuchura** and are often filled with lamb.

The large **Taklamakan Desert** is warm (over 104°F/40°C) in summer and very cold (down to -4°F/-20°C) in winter.

The Buddhist religion is the most widespread in western China, where **colorful prayer flags** are flown in the sky.

Tibet is home to five of the 14 tallest **mountains** in the world.

The deity **Mahākāla** is usually portrayed as black with six arms and is worshipped in many religions. Tibetan Buddhists believe he is the fierce guardian of the laws of nature.

The **Potala Palace** in Lhasa is a sacred site for Tibetan Buddhists.

The **yak** is large ox that lives in high altitudes. It's used to carry heavy loads and is a source of clothing, food, and fuel.

Wheat **noodles** form the base of many dishes in northern China, while in the south, the staple food is rice.

The **Emin Minaret** is a mosque in the city of Turfan in the mostly Islamic region of Xinjiang, which was conquered by China in the 18th century.

The **Chinese dragon** is a strong, positive symbol of control and power. It was a symbol of the Chinese Empire.

The **covered wagon** and the **buffalo** have been part of the Chinese landscape for centuries.

The **Jiayu Pass** was built in the 14th century at the western end of the Great Wall of China, which begins thousands of miles to the east in Laolongtou.

The **Yangtze**, or "Long River," is 3,915 miles (6,300 km) long, making it the longest river in China.

Rice was first grown in China more than 13,000 years ago. Today it's a staple food in many parts of the world.

The beautiful, decorated **bronze vases** made in China 4,000 years ago are important ritual objects and symbols of power.

The **taotie** is a monstrous animal from Chinese myths that is sometimes found on the oldest Chinese bronze artifacts like vases and bowls.

The classic **Chinese paper lantern** is usually red, which is the color of joy and good fortune for the Chinese people.

Qin Shi Huang was an emperor who unified China 2,200 years ago. Researchers have found thousands of **warrior soldier statues** around his tomb.

The **Giant Wild Goose Pagoda** was built 1,300 years ago. A pagoda is a traditional Chinese tower.

The **giant panda** produces very few cubs and eats bamboo.

China is creating **robots** that can work in factories, in your home, or even as dentists.

In the province of Guizhou there are **terraces** that are used to grow rice. These terraces are like steps that were built into mountains or hills many years ago.

Another important tourist attraction in China is the **mountains of Guangxi**, large chalk cliffs that rise up from the rice fields.

The **South China tiger** is probably extinct in the wild, and the last of the species live in two protected reserves in southern China.

 The **Harbin International Ice and Snow Sculpture Festival**, which takes place in cold northeastern China, attracts artists from all over the world, whose beautiful sculptures will all eventually melt.

 The Hakka population of southeastern China built circular, walled villages that act like fortresses to defend itself from its **neighbors**.

 The **Leshan Giant Buddha** is 233 feet (71 m) tall and is a statue of Maitreya, the future Buddha who has not yet been born.

 The **red-crowned crane** is a character in many Chinese legends and a symbol of long life.

 The **junk rig sailboat** is the typical Chinese ship. It's believed that 2,200 years ago, some of them were big enough to carry 700 people and 260 tons of cargo!

 Green tea comes from China, where it's been used for centuries as a medicine.

 An Italian painter named Giuseppe Castiglione painted portraits of the **emperors** of the last Qing dynasty in the 18th century.

 Bruce Lee is considered to be the king of kung fu. He grew up in Hong Kong and is an important unofficial ambassador of Chinese culture in the world.

 Like other noblemen of his time, the prince **Liu Sheng** was buried more than 2,000 years ago in a "suit" made of pieces of jade, a green gemstone.

 The **bridge** on Xinghai Bay in the city of Dalian is one of the many new bridges built in China in the last few years.

 A giant statue **Guan Yin**, the Chinese goddess of mercy, stands on the island of Hainan, which is the smallest and southernmost province of China.

 In China steam trains are still used to pull **train carriages** along the Trans-Mongolian Railway.

 Powerful **stone lions** guard the entrances to the Forbidden City in Beijing, which was the last home of the Chinese emperors. Today it is a museum.

Taiwan

 The **Taipei 101** skyscraper in the capital of Taipei is 1,667 feet (508 m) tall and has 101 floors.

 The areas around Beijing are home to some of the most beautiful sections of the **Great Wall**, which is more than 3,885 miles (6,250 km) long.

 The philosopher **Confucius** lived about 2,500 years ago. His teachings are still important to China.

 People with scary faces and brightly **painted faces** represent celestial beings and mythical characters during many festivals in Taiwan.

 A big monument with two large heads is in the city of Holingol. It is a tribute to the **Mongolian warriors** who conquered most of Asia centuries ago.

 Fireworks were invented in China, where they've been made for 1,300 years to celebrate holidays and drive away spirits.

 One of the most important festivals in Taiwan takes place at the beginning of the summer when the rowers of the long, colorful **dragon boats** have speed contests.

North Korea

 Fossils of unknown species of **dinosaurs** were discovered several years ago in Inner Mongolia.

 A giant statue of **Shennong**, considered the founder of farming in China, is in the Shennongjia Forestry District in the province of Hubei. The reserve is full of rare species of plants and animals that mostly live in forests.

 The **Arch of Reunification** is in the city Pyongyang. Its two female figures represent the government's efforts to reunite North and South Korea.

 The province of Heilongjiang has a cold climate and is home to many **spruce-fir** forests.

 The city **Shanghai** is home to 139 skyscrapers and 24 million people.

 Tonghae Satellite Launching Ground is a rocket-launching site in North Korea's North Hamgyong Province.

South Korea

 Namsan Tower is one of the symbols of the capital of Seoul and an important tourist attraction. It's 775 feet (236 m) tall, but towers almost 1,575 feet (480 m) over the capital because it stands on a hill.

 Korea, like nearby China and Japan, has produced beautiful green porcelain stoneware known as **celadon** for years.

 The **gat** is a tall Korean hat made of horsehair and bamboo.

Japan

 Sumo wrestling is the ancient style of wrestling that is Japan's national sport.

 Japan is the birthplace of high-speed trains. The legendary **Shinkansen** train can reach up to 200 miles (320 km) per hour.

 In Japan there is a unique colony of **macaque** monkeys that live in the forests in summer and in the hot springs of Jigokudani in the winter.

 Mount Fuji is a volcano 12,388 feet (3,776 m) high that has been dormant for 300 years. It is a symbol of Japan and a sacred mountain for the Japanese.

 A **torii** is a wooden structure that is usually red. It is considered a "gateway" to a sacred space in the Japanese Shinto religion.

 Manga are Japanese comic strips that are popular all over the world. Some, like Mazinger, feature super robots.

 Geishas are traditional female Japanese entertainers. They play classical Japanese music, dance, and recite poetry.

 In Japan, cherry blossom viewing is a national custom called **hanami**. For many Japanese, it's an occasion to go on walks and picnics.

 Sushi was invented centuries ago as a way to preserve fish. It is now eaten all over the world.

 Samurais armed with sharp **katana** swords were the early warriors of Japan. They were also men of culture, poetry, and letters.

Myanmar

 The **Chinthe** is a mythical half lion and half griffin that is well-loved by the people of Myanmar. They often stand guard at the entrances of temples.

 The **Shwedagon Pagoda** in Yangon is 344 feet (105 m) tall and is entirely covered in gold.

 In the city of **Bagan** there is a forest of **stupas**, or Buddhist monuments, which are about 1,000 years old.

 The many **hill tribes** that live in Myanmar have unique practices, like lengthening women's necks with metal rings.

Thailand

 The **Golden Buddha** is a giant gold statue in the city of Bangkok. It is more than 9 feet (3 m) tall and weighs 5.5 tons (5,500 kg).

 In Thailand the **elephant** is a symbol of strength and generosity and is considered a sacred animal.

 As in China and all of Southeast Asia, **rice** is a staple food in Thailand.

 In the north and northeast regions of Thailand, the long-horned **buffalo** is used both for meat and to pull the farm wagons that are still in use.

 The **dugong** is a marine mammal that is related to the cow. It grazes on the seagrass in the water around Thailand.

 The Andaman Sea is surrounded by beautiful **cliffs**.

Laos

 The **Wat Xieng Thong** is a Buddhist temple that has roofs with an upward-curving shape placed one on top of the other.

 The statues in **Buddha Park** in the north of Laos look very old, but were built in 1958. The humidity of the forest has aged them and made them look timeless.

 In the **Angkor Wat** mountain temple, giant heads represent the Buddhist god of Avalokiteśvara, who is always ready to help humanity.

 Dancers take years to learn all the steps and gestures of traditional **Cambodian dances**.

Vietnam

The beautiful **Ha Long Bay** is full of dozens of limestone islands that look like they're suspended between the sea and the sky.

The **whale shark** is the biggest fish in the world and can be found in the waters around the Philippines. It's as long as a bus (40 feet/12 m) but only eats microscopic creatures.

The **flying snake** climbs trees and jumps onto its prey to poison and eat it.

Kites have been made in Vietnam for many centuries, and today it is home to an international festival in which hundreds of colorful kites in every shape and size are flown.

Malaysia

The **Petronas Towers** in Kuala Lumpur, the capital of Malaysia, are 1,483 feet (452 m) high and connected by a bridge 561 feet (171 m) off the ground.

Indonesia – Java

The **Borobudur** temple, located on the Indonesian island of Java, is one of the biggest monuments in the world. It is six levels high and decorated with hundreds of Buddha statues.

Vietnamese junk boats are sometimes used as houses by people living on the coast.

There are four species of **sea turtles** living in Malaysia. Some of them are almost extinct, while others are slowly returning from near extinction thanks to conservation efforts.

Indonesia – Bali

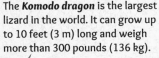

The **Komodo dragon** is the largest lizard in the world. It can grow up to 10 feet (3 m) long and weigh more than 300 pounds (136 kg).

The incredible **Dragon Bridge** at Da Nang in Vietnam is 2,185 feet (666 m) long and spits fire on Saturday and Sunday nights.

The **Rafflesia** is the biggest flower in the world and can be found in Malaysia. It grows up to 3 feet (1 m) in diameter and 22 pounds (10 kg) in weight.

Indonesia – Kalimantan

The **orangutans** are red-haired apes that are one of mankind's closest relatives. Their name means "humans of the forest."

Philippines

Large steps called **terraces** were built into the hillsides to grow rice on the island of Luzon.

The **rhinoceros hornbill** is a bird that is similar to the toucan, with a large yellow beak and a red "horn" on its head, which looks like the horn of the great African mammal it is named after.

Indonesia – Sulawesi

Banggai cardinalfish, which live in the waters of the island of Sulawesi, have long fins and a forked tail.

The **Mayon Volcano** is part of the Pacific Ring of Fire, which is made up of active volcanoes on the borders of the Pacific Ocean.

Brunei

The Istana Nurul Iman is the **Sultan of Brunei's palace** and is in the city of Bandar Seri Begawan, the capital of Brunei. It is the world's largest residential palace.

Western New Guinea

The **Asmat** people of Western New Guinea wear a mask that covers their entire body after funerals for family and friends.

Singapore

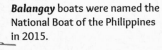

Balangay boats were named the National Boat of the Philippines in 2015.

The **merlion** is a mythical creature with the head of a lion and the body of a fish, depicted in fountain-statues that represent the country and city of Singapore.

Indonesia – Sumatra

Large, colorful **butterflies** of Indonesia live in the forests and many of them are endemic, meaning they are found only in the one area of the planet from which they come, and nowhere else.

The **Philippine tarsier** is a small mammal that lives in the trees and feeds on insects. Its large, round eyes help it to see at night.

Population:
1.2 billion

Surface area:
18.6 million square miles
(30 million km²)

MOROCCO

TUNISIA

ALGERIA

LIBYA

WESTERN SAHARA

Med

CAPE VERDE

MAURITANIA

MALI

NIGER

CHAD

SENEGAL

THE GAMBIA

GUINEA-BISSAU

GUINEA

BURKINA FASO

SIERRA
LEONE

IVORY COAST

LIBERIA

GHANA

TOGO

BENIN

NIGERIA

CAMEROON

CENTRAL AFRICAN
REPUBLIC

SÃO TOMÉ AND PRÍNCIPE

EQUATORIAL
GUINEA

GABON

REPUBLIC OF THE CONGO

DEMOCRATIC REPUBLIC
OF THE C

ASCENSION ISLAND (UK)

SAINT HELENA (UK)

ANGOLA

NAMIBIA

Atlantic Ocean

Africa

anean Sea

EGYPT

SUDAN

ERITREA

DJIBOUTI

ETHIOPIA

SOMALIA

SOUTH SUDAN

UGANDA

KENYA

RWANDA

BURUNDI

TANZANIA

MALAWI

ZAMBIA

COMOROS

MOZAMBIQUE

MADAGASCAR

ZIMBABWE

MAURITIUS

SEYCHELLES

WANA

H AFRICA

SWAZILAND

LESOTHO

Arabian Sea

Indian Ocean

Link to download the map:

https://www.hachettebookgroup.com/africa

65

Africa
The Center of the World

Africa is divided almost exactly in half by the equator (0° latitude) and is crossed by the Greenwich meridian, from north to south. So, in a way, it's the center of the world.

The continent is actually moving at a speed of ¾ inch (2 cm) per year toward Europe and Asia, continuing to push them and creating mountains like the Alps.

Despite its solid appearance, Africa is splitting along a line called the East African Rift, a valley six times the length of Italy that marks the point where East Africa is breaking away from the rest of the continent.

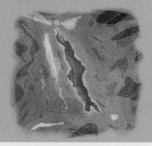

Africa is very old and has had a lot of time to create a rich geological heritage. It is full of natural resources like diamonds, oil, uranium, copper, and gold.

Africa is for the most part composed of plains or flat areas, but it also has mountain chains and peaks like Kilimanjaro in Tanzania, which is the highest mountain in Africa.

From these mountains and often active volcanoes, come two of the greatest rivers in the world, the Nile and the Congo, which bring life to a continent that is home to some of the hottest points on the Earth. Both the biggest and the oldest deserts in the world, the Sahara and the Namib, are found in Africa.

Africa has some very special features, like the Eye of the Sahara, a spiral-shaped dome 25 miles (40 km) wide in the desert. The beautiful Lake Natron in Tanzania is made of very salty water the color of fire.

Africa's waters fill deep lakes like Tanganyika (4,710 feet/1,436 m) and create natural wonders like Victoria Falls, the largest waterfall in the world. The lakes and rivers keep forests like the Congo green and keep the extraordinary flora and fauna of this continent alive.

Incredible plants grow in Africa, like the baobab, the quiver tree, and the dragon tree. Fascinating animals like the elephant, lion, giraffe, rhinoceros, and hippopotamus live there, as well as our closest relatives, the chimpanzees and the last gorillas on the planet.

Scientists believe that our species, *Homo sapiens*, was born in what is now Ethiopia and spread across the globe to all continents except Antarctica.

Africa has been inhabited by humans for longer than any other place in the world. In fact, African populations are famous for the variety of their costumes, customs, and languages (there are believed to be about 3,000 different languages!).

There are many old civilizations in Africa, such as Ancient Egypt and African kingdoms and empires like Nok in Nigeria (3,500 years ago) and Great Zimbabwe (600 years ago).

There are many different groups of people in Africa. The Berbers live in the north, while the Zulu and the Maasai people live in the south.

Africa has maintained its own traditions better than other parts of the world. Detailed tribal masks pass down beliefs from generation to generation. In Africa, religions like Christianity and Islam coexist with ancient beliefs like animism, which worships the spirits of nature.

Music and dance from Africa have deeply influenced the culture of the modern world.

Although it has many deserted areas like the Sahara, Africa is a hugely populated continent and home to modern cities like Lagos in Nigeria and Cairo in Egypt, with over 18 million people.

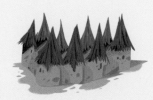

Thanks to the hot, tropical climate, products that are eaten all over the world, like bananas, pineapples, coffee, and cotton, are grown in areas of Africa.

Besides the important raw materials, tourism is also a source of income for many African countries. In the north, thousands of visitors admire the pyramids. Safaris attract tourists searching for elephants and lions south of the Sahara desert.

Algiers

Tunis

TUNISIA

Rabat

MOROCCO

ALGERIA

Canary Islands

Santa Cruz
de Tenerife

Laayoune

WESTERN
SAHARA

NIGER

CAPE VERDE

Nouakchott

MAURITANIA

MALI

SENEGAL

Dakar

Praia

Niamey

THE GAMBIA

Banjul

GUINEA-
BISSAU

Bissau

GUINEA

Bamako

Ouagadougou

BURKINA FASO

BENIN

Abuja

Conakry

Freetown

SIERRA
LEONE

IVORY COAST

Yamoussoukro

TOGO

NOLLYWOOD

NIGERIA

Monrovia
LIBERIA

GHANA

Accra

Lomé

Porto-Novo

CAMEROON

Yaoundé

Northern
Africa

Atlantic Ocean

68

Mediterranean Sea

Tripoli

LIBYA

EGYPT

Cairo

SUDAN

Khartoum

CHAD

N'Djamena

ERITREA

Asmara

DJIBOUTI

Djibouti City

Addis Ababa

CENTRAL
AFRICAN REPUBLIC

Bangui

SOUTH
SUDAN

Juba

ETHIOPIA

SOMALIA

Mogadishu

Indian Ocean

Northern Africa

Algeria

The Maqam Echahid, or **Martyrs' Memorial**, is a monument in the capital, Algiers, that shows three palms beneath which burns the Eternal Flame of independence.

Tassili n'Ajjer is a national park in the Sahara desert. Twelve thousand years ago, herdsmen and hunters left beautiful **rock paintings** in some of the caves.

Northern Africa is the last place in the world where **caravans**, or groups of people traveling together, are still trading and transporting goods across the desert.

Great **ammonites**, now fossilized, were shelled marine animals that used to live in the shallow sea that covered the western Sahara 350 million years ago.

Oddly shaped rocks stand on **Assekrem**, a young volcanic plateau—an area high above the ground—that formed only 2 million years ago.

The **horned viper** is poisonous. If it is disturbed, it will make a noise by rubbing its scales together.

Morocco

The **Hassan Tower** is 140 feet (44 m) high and is in the Moroccan capital, Rabat. It was intended to be the highest minaret (which is a thin tower) in the world, but construction was stopped in 1199.

Fantasia is a horse show in Morocco. Skilled horsemen and Arabian horses charge in a straight line before shooting old muskets into the sky.

In Morocco, artisans make old-style curved **daggers**, similar to those used by the Caliph armies that conquered the region 1,400 years ago.

Water sellers wear big hats to help block the hot sun in Morocco.

The **Tuaregs** are herdsmen and nomadic traders of the desert who were the first to use Arabian camels as transportation.

The terracotta tagine (**tajine**) pot cooks food in a healthy way. It is very common in Morocco.

The **Hassan II Mosque** in Casablanca has the highest minaret, or thin tower in the world. It is 690 feet (210 m) tall.

Western Sahara

Laayoune is the largest city in the territory of Western Sahara.

Tunisia

The **Medina** is an ancient part of the city of Tunis. It is 1,000 years old and home to 100,000 people.

The **Great Mosque of Kairouan** was built in AD 670, making it one of the oldest in the world.

The **Amphitheatre of El Jem** is like Rome's Colosseum, but smaller. It was built in the 3rd century AD and could hold 35,000 people.

Ghorfas were vaulted rooms used by the Berber people to store food supplies in cities like **Medenine**.

Beautiful wool **carpets** are made in Morocco.

Libya

Tripoli Tower is a 393-foot (120 m) tower and skyscraper in the capital city of Tripoli. Its former name, Al Fateh, means "young."

The Libyan desert is home to numerous **oases**, which are areas in the desert where water is found. Some cities and villages are built on oases.

Leptis Magna was a Roman city in the 3rd century AD. It was one of the last cities of the empire to succeed.

The Sahara is home to more than 30 species of scorpion. They can survive a year by eating only a couple of insects.

Tents made of dark cotton that can be used in both hot and cold weather are still commonly used as housing by the Bedouin people.

Libya has the biggest **oil deposits** in Africa.

The Greeks founded the ancient city of **Cyrene** 2,600 years ago. It has a temple bigger than the Parthenon in Athens.

Egypt

Pharaoh Ramesses II was a famous Egyptian pharaoh who lived 3,200 years ago. A statue of the leader measuring 36 feet (11 m) tall and 83 tons (75 metric tons) was found in 1820.

It takes about 15 hours to cross the 120-mile (193-km) **Suez Canal** by boat. If it didn't exist, you'd have to sail around Africa for days and thousands of miles.

The **Nile crocodile** can be up to 16 feet (5 m) long and is one of the last reptile species on Earth that give us an idea of what dinosaurs were like.

Egyptians believed they needed to preserve their bodies as **mummies** to make their journey to the afterlife.

The first **pyramid** was built 4,700 years ago. The pharaohs built many pyramids, but fewer than 100 still exist today.

The triangular sail of the **felucca boat** allows it to sail south up the Nile river and against the current, while to go north the boat can just follow the current.

The **Abu Simbel temple complex**, cut into the rock 3,200 years ago, holds four statues of Pharaoh Ramses II that are 65 feet (20 m) tall.

The **Nile hippopotamus** is now extinct in Egypt but is still considered a sacred animal. The god that protected children was a hippopotamus.

The **Red Sea** is the world's northernmost tropical sea and is home to hundreds of species of colorful fish and corals.

Mali

The **Peace Monument** in the capital city of Bamako features two hands holding a globe, on top of which is a dove, symbol of peace.

Five hundred years ago, the ancient city of **Timbuktu**, with its magnificent mud buildings, was a cultural and commercial center of legendary wealth.

The **djembe** is a traditional drum from Mali.

The Dogon farming people store their grain in **huts** with pointed roofs.

The Dogon are also famous for the huge **masks**, some 10 feet (3 m) high and supported by scaffolding, that they use in their ritual dances.

Gold is Mali's biggest natural resource and has been mined since the Middle Ages.

Acacia is a type of shrub or tree that can be found throughout the savanna in Africa. The savanna is a grassy plain that can be found in central Africa.

Niger

The **Grand Mosque of Niamey** is located in Niamey, the capital of Niger. Niger is a mainly Islamic country in western Africa.

The **Agadez Mosque** was built in the 16th century and is made of mud and reinforced with wooden poles that stick out of the walls.

Niger has some of the biggest **uranium deposits** in the world.

Niger is made up of plains in the north, mountains in the southeast, and a humid, grassy area in the southwest, which is home to herds of **long-horned cattle**.

Niger is home to the last **West African giraffes**, also known as Nigerian giraffes.

The country has the biggest population of **Tuareg** people. They are descendants of the famous nomadic people of the desert.

Chad

Our Lady of Peace Cathedral is in N'Djamena, the capital of Chad. Christianity is the second-biggest religion in Chad, after Islam.

The northern part of Chad is desert land and the southern part is the **savanna**. Savannas cover half of Africa and are wide-open spaces with some trees and bush.

The **Wodaabe** (or **Bororo**) people are nomadic cattle herders who carefully paint their faces to participate in a grand ceremony where the girls choose husbands.

Many species of animals that lived in the Saharan region before it became a desert sheltered in the shade of the strange rocks of the **Ennedi Plateau**.

Unique and colorful **mud buildings** with terraced roofs are seen in certain areas of Chad.

Canary Islands

The constant ocean winds around Grand Canary Island create perfect conditions for **paragliding**. The island is also home to Las Palmas, the capital of this archipelago province of Spain.

The Canary Islands are volcanic islands, and the biggest volcano, **Mount Teide** (12,198 feet/3,718 m), is the highest mountain in Spain, 1,056 miles (1,700 km) away from its motherland!

The mysterious **Pyramids of Güímar** on the island of Tenerife are very old, but nobody knows who built them or why.

Mauritania

Chinguetti was once a city rich in culture and commerce 1,000 years ago. Today, its fortified buildings have been taken over by the desert.

Gerbils live in the Mauritanian desert. About 75 percent of Mauritania is covered in deserts or semi-deserts.

Mauritanian women wear **malafas**, a long cloak wrapped around the body. Its length can vary depending on both the fashion and the women's hairstyles.

The **Eye of the Sahara** is a bizarre, spiral-shaped valley, 25 miles (40 km) wide and of mysterious origin. It may have been formed underground and then brought to the surface thanks to erosion.

Sudan

A building in the shape of a **ship's sail** in the capital city of Khartoum stands where the Blue Nile and White Nile rivers meet.

The **Meroë Pyramids** were built 2,300 years ago, in the time of the Kingdom of Kush.

The **Nile tilapia** is a large fish that lives in the Nile. It was first farmed 4,000 years ago and is still one of the most-eaten fish in the world.

Traditional straw huts are the most common type of housing in the remote **Nuba Mountains** in the southern part of Sudan.

The **black-necked spitting cobra**, found in the savanna of Sudan, spits its venom.

South Sudan

The **African fish eagle** is the symbol of this young nation, which was founded in 2011.

The **Mongalla gazelle** lives in South Sudan and can run up to 50 miles per hour (80 kph).

The mountains of the **Boma Plateau** are an important refuge for hundreds of thousands of **antelope** that migrate across the territory.

The women of the **Dinka** people wear corsets made with thousands of beads, especially red ones.

Eritrea

The **Enda Mariam Cathedral** in Eritrea's capital city, Asmara, was inspired by the architecture of the Kingdom of Aksum, which existed from AD 100 to 940.

The goats of the **Eritrean herdsmen** eat shrubs and live in the country's dry land.

Beautiful, natural fiber **baskets** are made in Eritrea and are used for many purposes, including trays, containers, and wallets.

Ethiopia

The **Lion of Judah** is an ancient symbol of the Hebrew tribe of Judah and of Ethiopia. Some of the people of Ethiopia descended from the Jewish tribe.

Brightly colored **icons**, or paintings, depict Christ with the same heavy braids worn by Rastafarians, the followers of a particular form of Christianity born in Ethiopia.

The **Obelisk of Axum** is 79 feet (24 m) high and may be the tombstone of some important people.

The bones of **Lucy**, an early human relative that walked on two legs more than 3 million years ago, were found near the village of Hadar.

Incense was a very precious product for all the ancient empires of the Mediterranean. It is created from the **myrrh** tree, originally from Ethiopia.

Coffee is also originally from Ethiopia and is currently the country's most exported product. The earliest evidence of coffee as a drink dates back 600 years.

Djibouti

Women of the Afar people from the small nation of Djibouti wear elegant **jewelry** similar to that worn by the Berbers of North Africa.

Somalia

African wild donkeys have legs like zebras. They live in Eritrea, Ethiopia, and Somalia.

Somali ostriches live in Somalia and Ethiopia. There are fewer of them in the wild today due to hunting and poaching.

The **banana** is an important product in Somalia and is exported to many countries around the world.

The **spotted hyena** feeds on dead animals but is also a skilled hunter of large animals such as the zebra.

Cape Verde

The brightly colored houses of **Praia**, the capital of Cape Verde, contrast with the dry landscape of this volcanic archipelago (group of islands).

The **Cape Verde giant gecko** lives only on the archipelago. It's a type of lizard and can be up to 1 foot (30 cm) long.

Senegal

The **African manatee** is a timid sea mammal that eats on seagrass along the west coast of Africa, from Senegal to Angola.

The **kora** is a string instrument played by the griots, Senegalese ballad singers who are very important to the country's culture.

The stocky trunk of the **baobab tree**, similar to a barrel, can contain thousands of liters of water to help the tree to survive in the dry climate.

The water of **Lake Retba** in Senegal is pink because of a specific kind of algae that lives in the lake.

The Gambia

Arch 22 in Banjul, the capital of The Gambia, looks like an arch but is also a three-story building with a museum inside.

Guinea-Bissau

The **Independence Pillar** in Bissau, the capital city of Guinea-Bissau, commemorates the end of colonialism in the country in 1973.

Mangroves are extraordinary trees that thrive in salt water. They can be found along the coast of Guinea-Bissau.

Guinea

The **Grand Mosque of Conakry** in Conakry, the capital of Guinea, can hold 25,000 people, making it one of the biggest mosques in Africa.

Farmers in Guinea grow many different kinds of crops, including rice, sweet potatoes, corn, bananas, and **pineapples**.

Diamonds are one of Guinea's most important resources. They are mined in the country's rain forest.

The **bushbuck** is a species of antelope that, unlike other kinds of antelope, isn't shy. It defends itself against leopards and other predators and even against hunters.

Sierra Leone

The **Mende** people of Sierra Leone believe that the spirit of their people resides in each one of their masks.

The **African rock python**, up to 16 feet (5 m) long, coils itself around tree branches to rest or to wait for prey like rodents, antelopes, and chickens.

Liberia

The Dan people of Liberia believe that the **masks** they wear allow the spirits of the forest to participate in the lives of the villagers.

Bananas and **coconuts** are important ingredients in Liberian cuisine.

There are many **leopards** in Liberia, but they're hunted for their meat, which is a common food.

Ivory Coast

Palm trees are an important resource in Ivory Coast. Oil and other useful substances are taken from the trees.

The Ivory Coast **national football team** is one of the best on the continent.

The small **pygmy hippo** still lives in the country. It's about four times smaller than the common hippopotamus and is in danger of extinction.

Ivory Coast's offshore **drilling platforms** extract oil and natural gas, which are important resources for the country.

Ivory Coast is the world's largest producer of **cacao**, which is used to make chocolate.

Ghana

The **Independence Arch** in Accra, the capital of Ghana, stands in Black Star Square, the second-largest city plaza in the world.

The **panther** is a leopard with black fur rather than spots. In Ghana, it lives wild but also has contact with humans.

The kings of the **Ashanti** people sit on the Golden Stool, a throne so sacred that only they can touch it. It is believed that the spirits of the nation live inside it.

The **Akosombo Dam** has created the biggest man-made lake in the world and provides electricity for Ghana's aluminum industry.

Togo

Guenons are small monkeys with white beards that live in Togo and nearby countries in Africa.

Burkina Faso

Ouagadougou, capital of Burkina Faso and former capital of the Mossi Kingdoms, has interesting architecture that is a mix of modern and colonial.

The **houses of the Tamberma people** of Burkina Faso are miniature castles with turrets from top to bottom. They once defended the people against their enemies and today they make good shelters from the heat.

While **sugarcane** is grown in Burkina Faso, farming is difficult in the country due to droughts.

Benin

This rare **ivory mask** depicting Idia, an ancient queen of Benin, is worn not over the face but around the neck like a pendant.

Cotton is an important product for countries bordering the Gulf of Guinea like Benin, and it's exported all over the world.

Nigeria

Modern skyscrapers stand in the center of **Lagos** in Nigeria, a city with 16 million people, making it the second-largest in Africa after Cairo.

Nigeria has the richest economy of the continent, thanks to its natural resources like oil and tin.

The Nigerian cinema industry, called **Nollywood**, makes more movies than Hollywood each year.

The **baboons** of the savanna live on the ground and not in the trees. They make vowel sounds similar to humans and can recognize written words.

Cameroon

The spiral-shaped Reunification Monument in Yaoundé, the capital of Cameroon, represents the **reunification** of the two colonies, one British and one French, that divided Cameroon until 1972.

The **Mafa** people in Cameroon live in huts that look like small towers. Inside they have bedrooms, kitchens, granaries, storerooms, and stables.

Heavy **trains** run on the only railway line in Cameroon, which connects the large Port of Douala with the inner areas of the country.

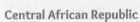

The **balafon**, a typical West African instrument, is made from hollowed gourds and hard wooden keys that produce a metallic sound.

Central African Republic

The great **tropical rain forests** of the African continent are in the southern park of the Central African Republic.

The **savanna** is in the northern part of the country.

Giraffes, which live in most parts of Africa south of the Sahara, may look the same, but in reality their spots are quite different depending on the region.

Gazelles can be found all over Africa, where they are protected or hunted depending on the country. In the Central African Republic, however, they're unfortunately in danger of extinction.

Vividly colorful **butterflies** can be found in the country's humid forests, and some of them have wings that stretch almost a foot (30 cm) wide.

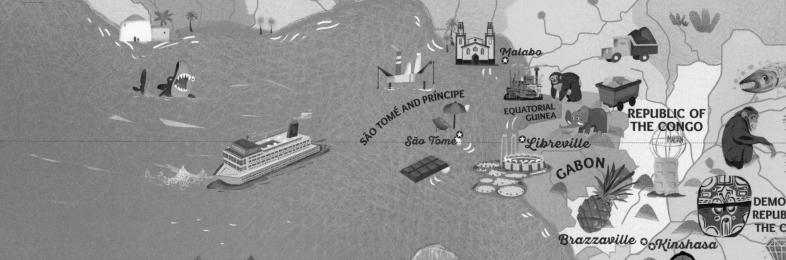

Malabo ☆

São Tomé and Príncipe

EQUATORIAL GUINEA

São Tomé ☆

REPUBLIC OF THE CONGO

☆ Libreville

GABON

DEMOCRATIC REPUBLIC OF THE CONGO

Brazzaville ☆ ☆ Kinshasa

Atlantic Ocean

☆ Luanda   ANGOLA

SAINT HELENA

☆ Jamestown

NAMIBIA

BOTSWANA

☆ Windhoek

Southern Africa

Link to download the map:

https://www.hachettebookgroup.com/southern-africa

74

UGANDA

KENYA

Kampala

RWANDA

Kigali

Nairobi

Bujumbura BURUNDI

SEYCHELLES

Victoria

Dodoma

TANZANIA

COMOROS

Moroni

Indian Ocean

ZAMBIA

MALAWI

Lilongwe

MOZAMBIQUE

Lusaka

Antananarivo

MAURITIUS

Port Louis

Harare

ZIMBABWE

MADAGASCAR

Gaborone

Pretoria

Maputo

Mbabane

SWAZILAND

Maseru

LESOTHO

SOUTH
AFRICA

Southern Africa

Uganda

Lake Victoria is the biggest lake on the continent and the biggest tropical lake in the world.

The best places to see **zebras** in Uganda are Lake Mburo National Park and Kidepo Valley National Park.

Cheetahs live all over Southern Africa. They are the fastest big cats and can run up to 71 miles per hour (114 kph).

Coffee is the most important crop in Uganda.

Kenya

The **Kenyatta International Convention Centre (KICC)** is a 28-story building in Nairobi, the capital of Kenya, and is the headquarters of many government offices.

The **Maasai** are a tribal people who live on the border between Kenya and Tanzania.

Tourists ride in **jeeps** when going on **safaris** in the national parks of Southern Africa, hoping to see elephants, giraffes, lions, and other animals in the wild.

Kenya has 333 miles (536 km) of coastline and many beautiful **beaches** with bright white sand.

The **Turkana Boy** is the almost complete skeleton of a hominid, a relative of humans that lived in Kenya 1.6 million years ago. It was discovered near Lake Turkana.

São Tomé and Príncipe

São Tomé and Príncipe was the largest producer of **cacao**, the seed used to make chocolate, in the early 1900s. They were nicknamed "the chocolate islands."

These small, lush islands off the coast of West Africa still have **untouched beaches**.

Equatorial Guinea

San Fernando Church in Malabo, the capital of Equatorial Guinea, is one of the city's main tourist attractions.

Gorillas live all over Southern Africa. Even though they are very big and strong, they are usually peaceful and calm animals.

One of the principal economic activities in Equatorial Guinea is the **chemical industry**.

Equatorial Guinea is the richest country in Africa thanks to its many **oil rigs**, but this wealth is distributed among only a few powerful families.

Gabon

In 1839, France took over Gabon. The name of the capital, **Libreville** ("free town"), dates back to 1849 when French troops freed the slaves.

The main economic activity in Gabon is the **mining** of iron and gold.

The **African forest elephant** lives in the rain forest and is smaller than its cousin in the savanna.

Republic of Congo

Mbandaka is a city in the Republic of Congo that is on the equator. There is a landmark on the **"latitude zero"** point.

The **pineapple** is originally from South America but is also grown in Southern Africa.

Democratic Republic of the Congo

In the Democratic Republic of the Congo, long **masks** are made to ward off evil spirits and also to hide the faces of members of secret societies.

The **bonobo**, also called the dwarf chimpanzee, lives in the rain forests south of the Congo River. It's the only place in the world that these animals can be found in the wild.

The mines of the Democratic Republic of the Congo are rich in precious metals like gold, copper, and **diamonds**.

The **okapi** is the only living relative to the giraffe. It lives in northern, central, and eastern parts of the Congo and has reddish brown or purple fur with striped legs.

The beautiful **Saints Peter and Paul Cathedral** in the city of Lubumbashi was inspired by the basilicas in Ravenna, Italy.

The **tiger fish** is a large freshwater fish commonly found in African lakes and rivers. It gets its name from its sharp teeth and aggressive behavior.

Different species of monkeys and elephants can be found in the **savannas** of the Congo.

The **giraffe** is the tallest living land animal in the world thanks to its long neck and slender legs, which allow it to eat the leaves of the savanna trees.

Zanzibar is a group of islands off the east coast of Tanzania that is famous for its beautiful beaches and its variety of spices.

Angola's national **basketball** team is one of the best African sports teams.

Rwanda

The Teke people use **Teke masks** that have a bar on the back to be held between the teeth during ceremonies.

Mount Kilimanjaro in northeast Tanzania is 19,341 feet (5,895 m) high, making it the highest mountain of Africa.

The unique, horn-shaped headgear worn by women of the **Herero** tribe comes from 19th-century European fashion, back when Africa was colonized.

The Tour du Rwanda is a men's road **cycling** stage race that takes place in Rwanda every November.

Seychelles

The **Victoria Clocktower**, also known as Lorloz, is a national monument in Victoria, the capital of this small group of islands. It was named after Queen Victoria in 1903, when the United Kingdom ruled the region.

The **Southern African lion** is one of seven subspecies of lion. It's quite big and the males are blonder than their cousins.

Burundi

Peanuts, one of the most widely eaten foods in the world, are an important product in in Burundi.

The **sea coconut**, also known as the double coconut, only grows in Seychelles.

Zambia

The **Cathedral of the Holy Cross** in Lusaka, the capital of Zambia, is one of the most important works of modern architecture in Africa.

Tanzania

The masks of the **Makonde** people in Tanzania cover the entire head. Boys wear them during initiation rituals, ceremonies at the end of which they are considered adults.

Angola

The luxury **skyscrapers** built in the center of Luanda, capital of Angola, are part of what make it one of the most expensive cities in the world.

As it flows into a ravine 427 feet (130 m) deep, the Zambezi River creates one of the most impressive spectacles in the world: **Victoria Falls**, is the largest waterfall in the world.

Pink flamingo chicks are born at Lake Natron, the red salt lake full of algae that gives them their color.

Marlins are big fish that are very common in this part of Africa.

A replica black elephant is placed on top of the barge of the king of the Lozi people during the ceremony called **Kuomboka**, or "to get out of water" in Lozi, which celebrates the end of the rainy season.

The **Rally of Tanzania** is an international automobile racing event that was first held in 2001.

Angola has large **coffee**, cotton, tapioca, and sugarcane farms.

You can go on **walking safaris** in Zambia to get up close to elephants, rhinoceroses, and zebras.

Laetoli is an archeological site in Tanzania where **hominin (human relative) footprints** dating back almost 4 million years have been preserved in volcanic ash.

The **porcelain rose** is a plant grown in Angola and is also known as the pink porcelain flower.

Zambia's hot and humid climate is perfect for growing juicy fruits like **pineapples**, mangoes, and avocados.

Tanzania has natural resources of **gold**, gemstones, coal, and metals.

Angola is the fourth-biggest **diamond** producer in the world.

The **Maoma royal drums**, also known as Zambian drums, are very important to the Lozi people. They are seen as a symbol of strength and power.

Malawi

The **white-bearded wildebeest** lives in Southern Africa and travels in spectacular groups of hundreds of thousands.

Angola is the biggest producer of **gasoline** in Africa.

The children of the **Yao** people of Malawi and Mozambique wear costumes and masks during initiation ceremonies when they become adults.

Liwonde National Park, the biggest park in the country, is known for its *elephant* reserve.

There are hundreds of old ships stranded on the northern coast of Namibia, called the *Skeleton Coast*. The dense fog in the area makes it dangerous for ships.

 Southern yellow-billed hornbills live in Southern Africa and are called "flying bananas" because of their long yellow beaks.

 Tea, tobacco, and sugar are the main products of Malawi.

Botswana

 The *Christ the King Cathedral* in the capital city of Gaborone, with its twisted bell tower, is an interesting example of modern African architecture.

 Hippopotamuses spend most of their time in the rivers and lakes of Africa. Its name means "river horse" in Ancient Greek.

Namibia

 The *Christ Church* in the capital city was built in 1907 and designed by German architect Gottlieb Redecker. The clock and part of the roof was shipped to Africa from Germany.

 In 2016 the second-largest *diamond* ever found was discovered in Botswana. The largest diamond was found in 1905 in South Africa.

 The Shona people of Zimbabwe are famous for the art of stone *sculpting*, a modern technique in Southern African art.

Mozambique

 The *Sossusvlei* region in the southern part of the Namib desert has the highest sand dunes, or hills, in the world.

 Sunflowers, soybeans, and sugarcane are important products in the country's agriculture.

 Galagos, also known as bush babies, are small monkeys that live in the trees and feed on insects.

 The *elephants* of Namibia have learned to live in the desert and are nicknamed desert elephants.

 The *boomslang, or tree snake*, lives in the most humid areas of Southern Africa. They are very venomous but only attack if they feel they are in danger.

 The waters of Mozambique are full of fish and shellfish like lobsters, crabs, and *shrimp*.

 The *mountain zebra* is originally from southwestern Angola, Namibia, and South Africa. All zebras have different patterns of stripes. Scientists think they can tell each other apart by their stripes.

 Warthogs are a member of the pig family that mostly live in the savannas of Southern Africa. They can survive without water for more than six months.

 A large number of *rubies* were found in Mozambique in 2009. Now half of the world's rubies are mined in the country.

 Women of the *Himba* people of Namibia cover their bodies and hair in red clay to protect themselves against the hot sun.

 The semiarid region of Botswana is the land of the *Khoisan* people, also known as the Bushmen, hunter-gatherers who hunted animals for meat and gathered wild plants from the desert.

 The *Makonde* people of Mozambique create unique batik paintings that depict everyday life in their culture.

 Uranium was discovered in Namibia in 1928. The country provides 10 percent of all the world's production of the mineral.

Zimbabwe

 The airport in the capital city of Harare has a *control tower* inspired by traditional African architecture.

 The people of the Mozambique coast fish on boats with *triangular sails*.

Comoros

 Quiver trees are a large type of aloe tree that can only be found in Southern Africa. The tallest ones can be more than 300 years old.

 Great Zimbabwe is a medieval city and former royal palace with great stone walls that amazed the Europeans who discovered them.

 The arches of the *Old Friday Mosque* in the capital city of Moroni are typical of the architecture of the east coast of Southern Africa.

Mount Karthala is one the most dangerous volcanoes in the world. It has erupted more than 20 times since 1800.

Séga is a traditional form of music and dance of Mauritius. Its origins are a mixture of indigenous, European, Indian, and Chinese, just like the population of the country.

South Africa has many **cave paintings**, drawings of animals, humans, and spirits painted by hunters and herdsmen who lived thousands of years ago.

Madagascar

The **ravenala plant** is known as the traveler's plant because rainwater is collected at the base of its leaves. People drink from them after walking around in the hot Madagascan sun.

South Africa

The **Free State Stadium** in the city of Bloemfontein is one of the stadiums used by the national South African rugby team, the Springboks.

Nelson Mandela was the first president to be elected after the end of the apartheid, which was a system where nonwhites did not have the same rights as whites. He was awarded the Nobel Peace Prize in 1993.

Radiated tortoises are mostly found on the island of Madagascar. They can live more than 100 years.

The city of Stellenbosch is considered the **wine** capital of South Africa. The country is the ninth-largest wine producer in the world.

There is a museum dedicated to **windmills** in the Northern Cape, a windy region of the country that has large, dry plains.

Ring-tailed lemurs are part of the monkey family and live in southern Madagascar. They live in groups of seven to ten and are usually led by a female.

Pretoria is known as **Jacaranda City** because of the thousands of purple-blue-flowered jacaranda trees that grow there.

The **Cape fur seal** lives along the western coasts of South Africa. It is sometimes called the "dog of the ocean" because it's so curious and playful.

Ylang-ylang trees grow on Nosy Be, an island of Madagascar. The oil from their flowers is used to make perfumes.

The fossils of **Australopithecus africanus**, a relative of humans that lived 3 million years ago, were discovered in the Sterkfontein caves in 1935.

Surfing is a very popular sport along the many beaches of Cape Town, which are surrounded by powerful waves created by the meeting of the Atlantic and Indian Oceans.

Lesotho

Aloe polyphylla is a plant also known as spiral aloe because of the circular arrangement of its leaves.

The **red mangrove crab** lives in the mangrove trees in Madagascar. Along with the hermit crab, they are the only shellfish that climb trees.

The **greater kudu** is an antelope that lives in the wooded areas of Southern Africa. The males can be recognized thanks to their large, twisted horns.

Swaziland

The **blue vanga** is a beautiful blue bird that only lives on the African islands of Madagascar, Mayotte, and Comoros.

Meerkats are cute mammals that are only 20 inches (51 cm) tall. They are social animals that live in groups of up to 40 meerkats.

The **black mamba** is a dangerous snake that lives in the many parks and nature reserves of Swaziland. It's actually not black but brown, gray, olive, or khaki.

Mauritius

Manta rays have a wingspan of 18–23 feet (5.5–7 m) and can weigh up to 3,000 pounds. They can live in the wild for up to 50 years.

The **southern ostrich** lives in the wild in South Africa and is also raised by farmers for its meat, leather, and feathers.

Saint Helena

Jamestown is the capital of Saint Helena, an island belonging to the United Kingdom that was the final prison of **Napoleon Bonaparte** between 1815 and 1821.

The **dodo** was a bird from Mauritius that became extinct about 400 years ago because it couldn't fly, making it easy prey for predators.

The **Zulu** are the largest ethnic group in South Africa. They were once famous warriors who fought a series of wars with Great Britain.

The **arboreal fern** is the most popular plant on the island of Saint Helena.

Greenland
(DENMARK)

CANADA

Alaska
(US)

UNITED STATES

MEXICO

BAHAMAS

CUBA

JAMAICA

HAITI

DOMINICAN
REPUBLIC

PUERTO RICO (US)

BELIZE

GUATEMALA

EL SALVADOR

HONDURAS

NICARAGUA

COSTA RICA

VENEZUELA

Pacific Ocean

The Americas

Link to download the map:
https://www.hachettebookgroup.com/the-americas

Atlantic Ocean

SURINAME
French
Guiana
(FRANCE)

COLOMBIA

ECUADOR

PERU

BRAZIL

BOLIVIA

PARAGUAY

CHILE

ARGENTINA

URUGUAY

Inhabitants:
1 billion

Surface area:
16.4 million square miles
(42 million km²)

North America
Where the Sun Sets

The Americas are so large that they are two continents: North America and South America.

The Labrador Peninsula in Canada is one of the oldest parts of the world. Its solid rock islands came out of a sea of lava 3.9 billion years ago.

Until 100 million years ago, North America and Europe were part of one big piece of land called Laurasia. When tectonic forces split it in two, the North American plate moved to the west.

It then hit the Pacific plate, bending like a sheet of paper. The Rocky Mountains and the Coast Mountains of Alaska were created in the west, while in the east the continent remained flat, forming the Great Plains. The Appalachian Mountains, which are east of the Great Plains, had already been there for millions of years.

The eastern plains collected enormous quantities of water that ran from west to east, forming majestic bodies of water like the Mississippi River (2,340 mi/ 3,766 km), the Great Lakes, and Niagara Falls.

The continent's upside-down triangle shape creates a very particular climate. Most of the land is in the north, so it's cold. Polar regions like the tundra and the snow forests are home to moose, bears, and foxes.

In the south, the climate warms up, changing from the cold winters and hot summers of the Midwest to the mild climate of the East Coast and the subtropical climate of the North American deserts, like the Sonora in Mexico and the Mojave in the United States.

The climate and location of North America help create extreme weather conditions like the tornados of the Central Plains and the hurricanes in the Gulf of Mexico.

North America is full of beautiful trees like redwoods, which are the tallest trees in the world.

82

About 40,000 years ago, the oceans were hundreds of feet lower than they are today. Scientists believe that the lower water levels exposed land that is now covered in water, including the Bering Strait, which was a piece of land connecting North America and Asia.

Scientists believe the first groups of humans arrived in the Americas by crossing the Bering Strait, which would have been between the northeastern tip of Russia and what is now Alaska, searching for a new world. It took less than 10,000 years for humans to occupy North America, each group adjusting to the different environments in their own way.

The Arctic region in the north gave birth to the Inuit people, who lived by seal hunting, while in the Great Plains the Native Americans flourished, their lifestyle revolving around bison hunting.

Then, in 1492, European explorer Christopher Columbus landed in North America, and many more Europeans followed him.

Millions of immigrants arrived, attracted by the riches of the continent like gold, copper, uranium, coal, oil, and other natural resources. They created big cities like Chicago and New York, where the first skyscrapers in the world were built.

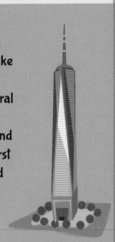

North America also helped create unique cultural heritages like jazz and blues, Hollywood cinema, the reign of Disney fairy tales, and the world's first food brands.

North America initially began to develop thanks to agriculture and animal raising, and then, thanks to big industries and global commerce. Today the continent's strongest industries are advanced technology and research.

Modern computer technology began in Silicon Valley in California in the 1970s, the Space Race took place in the '60s and '70s at Cape Canaveral in Florida, and environmental protection took its first steps here at the end of the 19th century with national parks like Yellowstone in the United States and Banff National Park in Canada.

North American baseball, football, basketball, and hockey teams are famous all over the world and contribute to the legend that is this continent.

Canada, Alaska, and Greenland

Arctic Ocean

ALASKA
(US)

Beaufort Sea

Pacific Ocean

YUKON

NORTHWEST TERRITORIES

Whitehorse

Yellowknife

BRITISH COLUMBIA

ALBERTA

Edmonton

SASKATCHEWA

Victoria   Vancouver   Calgary   Re

Link to download the map:

https://www.hachettebookgroup.com/canada-alaska-greenland

CANADA

GREENLAND
(DENMARK)

Baffin
Bay

NUNAVUT

Atlantic Ocean

Hudson Bay

MANITOBA

Iqaluit

NEWFOUNDLAND
AND LABRADOR

Saint John's

QUÉBEC

PRINCE
EDWARD
ISLAND

ONTARIO

NEW
BRUNSWICK

Charlottetown

Winnipeg

Québec City

Fredericton

Halifax

NOVA
SCOTIA

Montréal

Ottawa

Toronto

Canada, Alaska, and Greenland

United States – Alaska

The **moose** is the largest deer species in the world. The male can be up to 6.5 feet (2 m) tall, not counting its big horns.

The state of Alaska is home to more than 10,000 **wolves**.

Pioneers settled in Alaska in the late 19th century after the United States bought the land from Russia for $12.28 per square mile ($4.74 per km²).

Sasquatch or Bigfoot, the legendary monkey-man of the Northwest, is supposedly between 6.5 and 10 feet (2 and 3 m) tall.

Grizzly bears, or brown bears, are 8 feet (2.5 m) tall and can weigh between 300 and 1,500 pounds (136 and 680 kg).

Denali means "high one" in an indigenous language from the region and is 20,310 feet (6,190 m), making it the tallest mountain in North America.

Over 100,000 **people** migrated to Alaska after gold was discovered there in 1896.

Alaskan king crabs live in the cold waters around Alaska. They have a leg span of up to 6 feet (1.8 m) and weigh between 10 and 24 pounds (4.5 and 11 kg).

Killer whales create long-lasting social bonds and hunt in groups.

Greenland

The Inuit, an indigenous people in Greenland, hunts **caribou**, a North American species of reindeer, for food, clothes, and tools.

The **ski plane** is equipped with skates to stand on the snow.

The **national costume** of Greenland consists of leather boots, wool trousers, and wool jackets decorated with beads.

Erik the Red, a hostile Viking chief, was banished from Iceland, so he set sail and founded a settlement in Greenland that grew to 3,000 Vikings. One day, this community mysteriously vanished.

Years ago the colors of the **typical houses** of Greenland indicated the function of the buildings: red for the shops, yellow for the hospital, blue for the fishmongers.

The **polar bear** lives on Arctic ice and is considered a marine mammal. Due to global warming, there are only about 25,000 polar bears left in the world.

White in winter and grayer in the summer to camouflage, the **Arctic fox** feeds mostly on rodents like lemmings.

The **kayak**, a traditional boat the Inuit have been making for 4,000 years is made of sealskin and whalebones.

Canada – Yukon

With an average temperature of -16.6°F (-27°C), the top of **Mount Logan** (19,551 ft/5,959 m) has an ice cap, or large sheet of ice 984 feet (300 m) deep.

Over one billion dollars' worth of **gold** was found in the gold rush in Yukon.

Canada – Northwest Territories

Coal is Canada's most important energy resource. In 2014, the country supplied 0.9 percent of the world's production of this fossil fuel.

The **stone men, or inuksuk,** are like Inuit "road signs." They provide directions in the flat lands of the north.

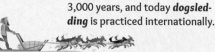
Dogsleds have been used for 3,000 years, and today **dogsledding** is practiced internationally.

The native nations of Canada write their histories and legends on **totem poles**, red cedar trunks that are carved into shapes, like eagles, bears, and wolves.

Canada – Nunavut

The **musk ox**, a relative of the goat, emits a strong odor during mating season to attract females.

The Royal Canadian Mounted Police (the **Mounties**) used to patrol on horseback, but now they use cars.

The **narwhal** is a type of whale. Males, and sometimes females, have a long tusk that can grow up to 10 feet (3 m) long.

Icebreakers push through thick sea ice with their hull, or the front of the boat, and are the most effective means of navigating the frozen waters of Canada.

During breeding season, **Atlantic puffins** return to the coast to lay eggs in cliffs, but otherwise they live alone in the ocean.

The **Pacific loon** yodels, growls, and barks.

After a fire, **St. Jude's Cathedral** in Iqaluit, Nunavut, was rebuilt in 2012 in the shape of an igloo.

Canada – British Columbia

Science World in Vancouver is a science museum that opened in 1985. It has the largest OMNIMAX screen in the world. It is a dome-shaped screen that is 81 feet (24.5 m) wide.

Many inhabitants of British Columbia belong to the **native nations, or indigenous tribes,** including the Haida, Coast Salish, Kwakwaka'wakw, Kitksan, Tsimshian, and Nisga'a.

The **Steller's jay**, which is similar to the blue jay, is symbolic of this province.

In the 18th century, Europeans came to British Columbia to sell the wood from **Douglas firs**, which were sometimes 1,000 years old and as big as soccer fields.

The jagged coastline of this region, formed by ancient volcanoes, is perfect for **kayaking**.

Every autumn, **salmon** use their impeccable sense of smell to migrate from the ocean to the same river where they were born.

Canada – Alberta

Lake Louise is a ski resort in the Banff National Park where the **Alpine Ski** World Cup races have been held.

Calgary was the first Canadian city to host the **Winter Olympics**, in 1988.

Every year in the province of Alberta, professional cowboys from all over the world compete in a **rodeo**.

The **Albertosaurus** was a small tyrannosaurid, similar to the T. rex, that lived in Canada 70 million years ago. It had sharp teeth, walked on two feet, and was at the top of the food chain.

The production of **electricity** in Canada is moving from coal to much more environmentally friendly sources.

Canada – Saskatchewan

The prairies of Canada have wheat, barley, sheep, and **cattle** farms.

Canada is the second-largest **uranium** producer in the world. Uranium is used for nuclear power.

Canada – Manitoba

About 1,000 **polar bears** live in the western part of Hudson Bay. The city of Churchill is called the Polar Bear Capital of the World.

In 1908, Manitoba was one of the first regions to utilize tractors to harvest grains.

The Native Americans on the Great Plains used **teepees** made of buffalo skins for shelter because they were easy to transport and adaptable to the climate.

Canada – Ontario

Wind turbines use the strong winds from the plains for energy.

Bison, also known as buffalo, were once close to extinction, but half a million roam Canada today.

The province of Ontario has many ponds, streams, and woodlands that make it perfect for **ducks**.

In the Great Lakes region, people **fish** for trout, panfish, walleye, salmon, bass, and the rare muskellunge, or muskie.

Seven of the world's largest car manufacturers have **assembly plants** in Ontario.

Sailing is the perfect sport for the Great Lakes because there are 11,000 miles (17,700 km) of coastline, dozens of ports, and great winds.

The most common tree in eastern Canada is the **red maple**. Its leaf is on the Canadian flag.

An international **hot air balloon** festival takes place in the province of Ontario.

At 167 feet (51 m) high, **Niagara Falls** is the most impressive waterfall in North America.

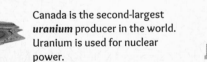

Parliament Hill, on the banks of the river in Ottawa, has been the meeting place of the Canadian parliament since 1876.

Canada – Québec

Château Frontenac is a famous hotel that opened in 1893 in Québec City, Québec, with more than 600 rooms and 18 floors.

The **forests** of Québec cover an area as large as Norway and Sweden combined.

The fur trade in North America almost made **beavers** extinct, but they have been saved and now there are almost a million in Canada alone.

The **golden eagle** is worshipped by native cultures across North America. They are the largest bird of prey on the continent.

Colonies of thousands of **gray seals** live on the shores of eastern Canada.

The **gray squirrel** is native to eastern Canada, but has spread to other countries.

The official bird of Québec is the **snowy owl**. Unlike most other owls, snowy owls are not nocturnal. They hunt in the daytime.

La Martre Lighthouse, in Gaspé, the peninsula in the southeast of Québec, was built in 1906 and is one of the many lighthouses that line the coast.

Canada – Newfoundland and Labrador

The waters around the island of Newfoundland are among the best in the world for **whale** sightings.

Fishermen sell **lobster** by the pound during lobster season.

Despite being big and heavy, the **Newfoundland** is a champion sea rescue dog.

The **snowmobile** is a modern version of the dogsled, but is much less environmentally friendly.

The **Labrador retriever** assists man in many ways, such as accompanying the blind, performing sea rescues, and searching for missing people.

The **Acadians** are the descendants of French colonists, who arrived in Canada during the 17th and 18th centuries.

Canada – New Brunswick

The first **lighthouse in Peggy's Cove**, one of the most famous tourist sites in Canada, was constructed in 1868.

Canada – Nova Scotia

The **Tall Ships Festival** celebrates that the city of Halifax is one of the stops on the international Tall Ship Regatta route, a historical boat race.

UNITED STATES OF AMERICA

Seattle
WASHINGTON

Portland
OREGON

MONTANA

NORTH DAKOTA

SOUTH DAKOTA

MINNESOTA

IDAHO

WYOMING

NEBRASKA

IOWA

NEVADA

Salt Lake City
UTAH

Denver

COLORADO

ROUTE 66

Kansas City

KANSAS

San Francisco
CALIFORNIA

AREA 51

Las Vegas

HOLLYWOOD
Los Angeles

OKLAHOMA

San Diego

ARIZONA

Roswell
NEW MEXICO

TEXAS

Dallas

El Paso

Pacific Ocean

San Antonio

Houston

Link to download the map:

https://www.hachettebookgroup.com/united-states

Continental United States

Lake Superior

WISCONSIN

Lake Michigan

Lake Huron

MICHIGAN

Detroit

Chicago

OHIO

ILLINOIS

INDIANA

Saint Louis

SOURI

KENTUCKY

Memphis

TENNESSEE

NSAS

MISSISSIPPI

LOUISIANA

ALABAMA

New Orleans

WEST VIRGINIA

Lake Ontario

NEW YORK

PENNSYLVANIA

Washington
(District of Columbia)

VIRGINIA

NORTH CAROLINA

SOUTH CAROLINA

Atlanta

GEORGIA

Charleston

Lake Erie

VERMONT

NEW HAMPSHIRE

MAINE

MASSACHUSETTS

Boston

CONNECTICUT

New York

RHODE ISLAND

NEW JERSEY

Philadelphia

DELAWARE

MARYLAND

BERMUDA (UK)

Atlantic Ocean

Orlando

FLORIDA

Miami

Gulf of Mexico

89

Continental United States

United States of America

WASHINGTON

The **Space Needle** is a symbol of Seattle. It is 605 feet (184 m) tall and has a revolving restaurant located 500 feet (152 m) above the ground.

The snowy, cold winters west of the Cascade Range are ideal for **skiing**.

OREGON

Oregon's large conifer trees (redwoods, Douglas firs, ponderosa pines) continue to supply a lot of timber, even though **forest felling, or cutting down trees**, has been reduced.

Albacore, a species of tuna, dive 1,300 feet (400 m) below the surface to eat. They also swim at 50 miles an hour (80 kph).

Fishermen harvest almost 55 million pounds (25 million kg) of **crabs** on the northwest coast every year.

Throughout the 19th century, the famous horse-drawn stagecoaches carried mail, valuables, and travelers along the **Oregon Trail**, 2,175 miles (3,500 km) between Missouri and Oregon.

CALIFORNIA

California is called the Golden State because the third **gold rush** of North America began here in 1848.

Mount Shasta is a dormant but active volcano that is a sacred place for many native communities and a landmark for Christians, Buddhists, and believers of other faiths.

In the 1970s California became part of the small group of the most prestigious **wine** producers in the world, and it now produces almost 90 percent of America's wines.

The tallest tree in the world is currently an evergreen **California redwood** (Sequoia sempervirens). It's 380 feet (115.8 m) high and located at the Redwood National Park.

The **Golden Gate Bridge**, the famous red bridge of San Francisco, stands 746 feet (227 m) above the water, and connects the San Francisco Peninsula to Marin County through Route 1.

In the 1960s California witnessed the birth of a fascinating sport: **extreme climbing** on smooth rock faces like the cliffs in the Yosemite Valley.

Thousands of Silicon Valley **digital technology** companies, including Apple, established themselves in this region of California 70 years ago because transistors were being produced in the area.

Intelligent, friendly, and even athletic, **California fur seals** are present in large numbers on the coast during breeding season.

In **Death Valley** in the Mojave Desert, the temperature often rises above 131°F (55°C) and there is very little rain.

The year 1911 marked the birth of **Hollywood** as the capital of cinema. Soon major film studios like Paramount, Warner Bros., RKO, and Columbia set up studios in the area.

Settlers of the gold rush harvested California **oranges** to fight scurvy, a disease caused by lack of vitamin C.

IDAHO

The state of Idaho is a **mountain biker's** paradise with 435 miles (700 km) of trails.

Yellowstone National Park spans the states of Idaho, Wyoming, and Montana and has geysers, bison, and **black** and **grizzly bears**.

NEVADA

The **pioneer wagons** followed the California Trail 3,000 miles (4,800 km) across Nevada in the mid-19th century.

Area 51, a top-secret military base, may study UFOs, but likely just develops military aircraft.

Las Vegas, a **gambling** capital, has resorts, casinos, entertainment, and nightlife all within the Mojave Desert in Nevada.

MONTANA

The wide plains of Montana, Kansas, and North Dakota are ideal for extensive farming. These areas are the biggest **wheat** producers in the country.

Fly-fishing is a popular sport in Montana. The fisherman or woman stands in the water dressed in special pants and boots.

While western Montana has steep mountains and deep valleys, nearly 60 percent of Montana consists of flat prairies, ideal for farming with **agricultural machinery**.

WYOMING

In the 19th and 20th centuries, **barns**, which are often painted red, allowed for the economic development of the prairies.

Devils Tower is a strange mountain of volcanic origin, made famous by the film *Close Encounters of the Third Kind*.

Like in Canada, the United States is slowly moving from coal to **renewable energy**.

UTAH
 Delicate Arch is a 60-foot (18 m) arch made of sand deposits that have been worn away by the wind over millions of years.

 In northwestern Utah, there is a large field called Bonneville Salt Flats covered in **salt** and other minerals. Cars, trucks, and motorcycles race on the salt at the Bonneville Speedway.

UTAH-ARIZONA
 Monument Valley is a desert region on the Arizona–Utah border with tall cliff-like formations called buttes. It has been used as a setting in many Western films.

ARIZONA
 Grand Canyon is a deep canyon, or valley, that is considered one of the seven wonders of the world. It is 277 miles (446 km) long and more than a mile deep.

 Geronimo, a famous leader of the Apache tribe, surrendered in 1886 to the American and Mexican militaries and was then forced to live on a reservation, a piece of land designated for Native Americans.

 The **saguaro**, a big cactus whose flower is the symbol of Arizona, is a robust plant that can live hundreds of years with very little water.

COLORADO
 Aspen, Colorado, is a famous **ski resort** city. It is 8,000 feet (2,438 m) above sea level.

 In **Tornado Alley**, an area that extends from Texas to Nebraska, the cold winds of Canada collide with the warm winds of Mexico to create devastating tornadoes.

 For centuries the spectacular cliff dwellings of **Mesa Verde** were home to the peaceful Ancestral Puebloans, skilled farmers and craftsmen who inhabited the region until about the 13th century.

NEW MEXICO
 Dolls with brightly colored masks and clothes created by the Hopi and other tribes, called **kachina dolls**, represent the spirits of nature, communicate between humans and the other world, and bring rain.

 Thick and juicy **T-bone steaks** are beloved in New Mexico.

NORTH DAKOTA
 The fields of North Dakota produce almost half of the **sunflowers** in the United States. Between August and September, the plains turn into a sea of bright yellow.

 Wild **Bill Hickock,** a shooter, spy, gambler, and hero in the Wild West, was shot while playing poker in 1876 in Deadwood, Dakota.

SOUTH DAKOTA
 The 60-foot (18-m) faces of presidents Washington, Jefferson, Theodore Roosevelt, and Lincoln took 14 years to carve into **Mount Rushmore**.

 The **Corn Palace** is an arena in the city of Mitchell, built in the 1920s and 1930s. The murals in the building are made out of corn and other grains.

NEBRASKA
 Chimney Rock, a large rock formation, was an extraordinary landmark for pioneer wagons heading west.

KANSAS
 Route 66 is more than 2,448 miles (3,940 km) long, and it crosses 8 states and 3 time zones.

 The **Niobrarasaurus** was an herbivorous armored dinosaur that lived 85 million years ago in the savannas of what is now Kansas.

 The **Kansas City Southern Railway** crosses the continent from Illinois to Mexico.

 Fast food was invented in the 1920s in Wichita, Kansas, where the first White Castle hamburger restaurant was opened.

OKLAHOMA
 Many **bison** roam wild in Oklahoma, where they have become one of the symbols of the state.

 The **Lexington Spider Beetle**, an old black Volkswagen in the shape of a gigantic spider, is a roadside attraction in the city of Lexington.

TEXAS
 Texas's economy depends on **livestock**, like the Texas Longhorn, a cow with large horns that is symbolic of Texas.

 After the gold rush in Alaska and California, the **oil** boom began in the 1920s in Texas.

MINNESOTA
 The **Mall of America** is the largest shopping center in America and has an amusement park, an aquarium, miniature golf, and many stores and restaurants.

 The **Paul Bunyan statue** celebrates the legend of the giant lumberjack, who, according to folklore, dug out the Grand Canyon.

IOWA
 The **Iowa Blue chicken** is a rare bird that may be a cross between a white hen and a pheasant.

MISSOURI
 The **Gateway Arch** is not only the largest arch in the world, but the largest man-made monument in the entire Western Hemisphere. It is located in St. Louis.

 Corn has been one of the main crops in Missouri since French settlers from Canada planted it nearly 300 years ago.

MISSISSIPPI
Square dancing originated in 16th- and 17th-century Europe, but followed European settlers to America and became a symbol of America's Wild West.

In 1812, the first *paddlewheel steamboat* sailed on the Mississippi River.

LOUISIANA
Alligator encounters are common in the swamps of Louisiana, and also in Georgia and Florida.

In the Mississippi Delta, large mossy trees grow in the *Atchafalaya Swamp*, the largest in the United States.

Mardi Gras, which means "Fat Tuesday" in French, was established in the 17th century by French settlers. It is a grand celebration that fills the streets of New Orleans in March.

WISCONSIN

A giant statue dedicated to the beloved *alien* E.T. welcomes travelers to Sparta, Wisconsin.

Wisconsin is called *America's Dairyland* because Wisconsin produces a quarter of America's cheese. People from Wisconsin and fans of the football team the Green Bay Packers are called Cheeseheads.

MICHIGAN

Turnip Rock is a fairytale-like island shaped into a cone by the waves of the Great Lakes. To prevent the rock from collapsing into Lake Huron, the base has been reinforced with concrete.

The Model T was the earliest affordable car. First produced in 1908, Ford's Model T was built using an assembly line, or a moving track in a factory, which lowered the price of the car and allowed more Americans to own cars and travel.

INDIANA

Since 1911, the famous *Indianapolis 500 race*, a *Formula One race*, and *Grand Prix motorcycle races* have been held at the Indianapolis Motor Speedway circuit.

The *Indiana University Hoosiers* are one of the best NCAA Division I college basketball teams in the nation and have won the National Championships five times.

ILLINOIS

If you like a lot of cheese and sauce, then you should visit Chicago and order *deep-dish pizza*, which has a thick, doughy crust topped with chunky tomatoes and gooey cheese.

Nuclear power is much cleaner than coal, oil, or gas because it doesn't hurt the environment, but if a nuclear power plant malfunctioned humans could be harmed. Illinois uses the most nuclear energy in the United States.

ARKANSAS

Arkansas has the only public park in the world where people can search for *diamonds*. Since 1906, people have been finding precious gems at Crater of Diamonds State Park.

ALABAMA

Enslaved Africans brought the *banjo*— which they made with a gourd—to the South in the 17th century and now it has become a common instrument throughout the region.

Some of the hottest *chili peppers* in the world come from this area of the United States.

FLORIDA

Disney World, a 48-square-mile (123 km^2) complex with four theme parks, two water parks, golf courses, and 28 hotels, opened in 1971.

Florida stone crabs don't only live in Florida. They can be found along the east coast of the United States and are caught for their deliciously large claws.

In the 1960s and 1970s, America launched spaceships and missiles from *Cape Canaveral* in the space race, when the U.S. competed with Russia to explore space.

SOUTH CAROLINA

Plantations were the houses where cotton and tobacco farm owners lived. Slaves, who worked all day in the fields, often lived in shacks.

NORTH CAROLINA

The Wright brothers built and flew the first plane in 1903 in Kitty Hawk, North Carolina.

VIRGINIA

Jamestown, Virginia, was the *first stable British colony* in North America, although the British people who came over to the New World faced hunger, thirst, and disease.

Wild turkeys can be found roaming the Virginia countryside. In Washington, D.C., which is close to Virginia, the president "pardons," or spares the life of, a single turkey every Thanksgiving.

WEST VIRGINIA

Coal is a rock that is mined from the ground and then used for fuel and heating. Coal mines provide many jobs in West Virginia, but can also harm people, animals, and the environment.

DELAWARE

In 1787, Delaware was the first state to sign, or "ratify," the *Constitution*, which is the document that guarantees America's freedoms.

MARYLAND

The *crab* is a symbol of Maryland. The Maryland blue crab loves the slightly salty water of the Chesapeake Bay and can live up to eight years.

TENNESSEE

Nashville is the capital of Tennessee and famous for its *country music*. In Nashville, country music stars play at the Grand Ole Opry House.

KENTUCKY
The Kentucky Derby, the first in a series of three horse races called the Triple Crown, is one of the most beloved horse races. Only twelve horses have won the Triple Crown in history.

Mammoth Cave is the largest cave system in the world, and is open to the public at a national park in central Kentucky.

GEORGIA, THE CAROLINAS, WEST VIRGINIA, KENTUCKY
Cotton, peanuts, and tobacco are three traditionally Southern crops. They grow well in a hot and humid climate.

GEORGIA
Georgia is also known as the Peach State because Georgians have been growing ***peaches*** since the 16th century.

The Masters Golf Tournament happens every April at the Augusta National Golf Club in Augusta, Georgia, and is one of the most important golf tournaments in the world.

OHIO
Baseball is the second most popular sport in the United States. The Baseball Heritage Museum is in the city of Cleveland.

Ohio is the Buckeye State because the ***buckeye*** is the state tree. People from Ohio are sometimes nicknamed Buckeyes.

PENNSYLVANIA
Professional football is the most popular sport in Pennsylvania, and the United States.

The ***Battle of Gettysburg*** was the turning point of the Civil War because the Union Army of the North won this violent but important battle.

CONNECTICUT
The ***Algonquin people*** are a large group of native American tribes who live along the Atlantic coast from Canada to Connecticut.

RHODE ISLAND
Rhode Island is called the Ocean State because the state has 400 miles (644 km) of coastline. Usually, ***horseshoe crabs*** crawl on the beaches.

MAINE
Vikings began exploring the North American coast in about AD 1000.

The ***blueberry*** is Maine's state berry—There are over 44,000 acres of wild berries that grow from late July to September.

Moosehead Lake is the largest lake in Maine and the largest mountain lake on the East Coast. Visitors fish for landlocked salmon, brook trout, and smallmouth bass in waters as deep as 246 feet (75 m).

MASSACHUSETTS
In 1773, the Americans who were living in the thirteen colonies threw an entire shipment of tea into the Boston Harbor to express anger with the British king, and eventually sparked the American Revolution.

In 1977, high school students spotted the ***Dover Demon***, a mysterious humanoid with long fingers and large eyes, in Massachusetts. Cree and Mohican folklore also have a similar creature.

At the end of the 17th century, a series of notorious ***witchcraft*** trials took place in the town of Salem, Massachusetts.

The very hungry caterpillar is one of the characters at the ***Eric Carle Museum***, an institution dedicated to children's picture books.

NEW HAMPSHIRE
Spruce trees, which can be used as Christmas trees, are found in the cold, mountainous regions of New Hampshire.

New Hampshire has many antique ***ice cream shops***, so it's no surprise they eat more ice cream than most other states in America.

NEW JERSEY
New Jersey is called the ***diner*** capital of the world because it has over 500 24-hour diners, which is the most diners in any state in America.

NEW YORK
New York grows more apple varieties than any other state, with 700 apple farmers, 10 million trees, and enough apples to make 500 million apple pies!

In the Marvel comic book, the character ***Spider-Man*** was born in Queens, a large and diverse borough in New York City.

One World Trade Center, the tallest building in the New York skyline, stands in place of the World Trade Center, which was destroyed on September 11, 2001.

The ***Statue of Liberty***, a gift from France, welcomed immigrants to America.

WASHINGTON, D.C.
The ***United States Capitol*** is where the U.S. Congress—the Senate and House of Representatives—creates laws.

George Washington became the first president of the United States in 1789 and remained in office for 8 years.

MEXICO

Gulf of Mexico

Pacific Ocean

Mexico City

Acapulco

BELIZE
Belmopan

GUATEMALA
Guatemala City

Tegucigalp

EL SALVADOR
San Salvador

Mana

Link to download the map:

https://www.hachettebookgroup.com/central-america

Mexico, Central America, and the Caribbean

BAHAMAS
★ Nassau

Sargasso Sea

Atlantic Ocean

★ Havana

CUBA

CAYMAN ISLANDS (UK)
George Town ★

JAMAICA
Kingston ★

HAITI
Port-au-Prince ★

TURKS
AND CAICOS (UK)
★ Cockburn Town

DOMINICAN
REPUBLIC
Santo ★
Domingo

BRITISH VIRGIN
ISLANDS (UK)
Road Town
PUERTO RICO (US)
San Juan ★   Charlotte
★ Amalie
U.S. VIRGIN
ISLANDS (US)

ANGUILLA (UK)
★ The Valley
★ Basseterre
SAINT KITTS
AND NEVIS
Plymouth
Basse-Terre
DOMINICA
Roseau

ANTIGUA
AND BARBUDA
Saint John's ★

GUADELOUPE (FR)
MONTSERRAT (UK)

MARTINIQUE (FR)

SAINT LUCIA
Castries
SAINT VINCENT AND
THE GRENADINES
Kingstown

BARBADOS
Bridgetown

Caribbean Sea

HONDURAS

NICARAGUA

San Jose
COSTA RICA

Panamá
City ★
PANAMÁ

ARUBA
Oranjestad ★
CURAÇAO
Willemstad ★

Kralendijk ★
BONAIRE (NL)

GRENADA
St. George's ★

TRINIDAD AND TOBAGO
Port of
Spain

Mexico, Central America, and the Caribbean

Mexico

The **Metropolitan Cathedral of the Assumption**, the largest church in the Americas, was built on the ruins of the Aztec temple Templo Mayor.

Mexicans decorate their family members' graves with colorful skulls, marigolds, and food for two days in late October and early November for the holiday **Día de Muertos**, the Day of the Dead.

In the Chihuahuan Desert there are **bones of a variety of different animals**, including deer, jaguars, and the rare pronghorn antelope, which can run as fast as 60 miles per hour (100 kph).

The Teotihuacán **Pyramid of the Sun**, 213 feet (65 m) high and 760 feet (230 m) long from the base, is one of the largest pyramids in Mesoamerica, or the region from Mexico to Costa Rica.

The duck-billed **Lambeosaurus** lived about 75 million years ago. It was 40 to 50 feet (12 to 15 m) long and its fossils have been found in Canada, the U.S., and Mexico.

The **Gila monster** is a poisonous lizard that is more than 18 inches (0.5 m) long. Unlike snakes, it injects its venom with its lower teeth.

The **Popocatépetl** (meaning the smoking mountain) and **Iztaccihuatl** (the sleeping woman) volcanoes, the first active and the second dormant, are more than 16,400 feet (5,000 m) tall and tower over Mexico City.

Tequila, a clear liquor, is made from the agave plant.

The extremely venomous **rattlesnake** lives all over the Americas from southern Canada to Argentina, but the largest number of species can be found in Mexico.

The **taco** is one of the most common foods in the world.

The **sombrero** was originally worn by **vaqueros**, Mexican cowboys, to protect them from the hot Mexican sun.

The hot and humid Yucatán Peninsula is partly covered by a dense **forest** that has become threatened by deforestation and cattle ranching.

The **mariachi band** typically consists of one guitar, eight violins, and two trumpets.

Agave, a very common type of plant with thick leaves, is native to Mexico.

Traditionally formed from hollowed gourds and then filled with pebbles or beans, **maracas** are traditional instruments in Mexico.

The **steel helmet** worn by the Spanish conquistadors, called a morion, was also used by the British because it was affordable to produce.

Cowboy boots are an important part of Mexican fashion, often made with rare animal hides and beautifully decorated.

The gray **whale** and the blue whale (and various other marine mammals) reproduce and spend the winter in the coastal lagoons of Baja California.

Living more than 3,000 years ago, the Olmecs, the first Mesoamerican civilization, carved large **stone heads** of their rulers out of volcanic boulders.

The **Dahlia pinnata, or garden dahlia**, is Mexico's national flower.

There used to be thousands of **pearls**, sometimes as big as eggs, in the waters of Baja California, but by 1940 most of them were gone from overharvesting.

Aztec kings like Montezuma wore **magnificent headdresses** made with the feathers of forest birds.

The **tomato** is native to Central America. For a long time Europeans thought it was poisonous, so it was initially grown as an ornamental plant.

In the Toltec and Mayan temples, offerings to the gods were placed on the stomachs of reclining figures, like the famous **Chacmool** sculpture.

The Maya people were an indigenous community who lived in Central America from AD 250–900. They were great mathematicians and astronomers and created a very complex *calendar*.

The *chili pepper* has been a basic ingredient in Mexican cuisine for centuries.

Guatemala

The *Popol Vuh Museum* is home to the most important collection of Mayan art in the world. This stone statue represents a bat.

Chocolate is made from the *cacao tree*. The ancient pre-Columbian populations who first cultivated it thought it was a gift from the gods to "sweeten" the hard life of men.

Central America has many *active volcanoes* that were created after the collision between the Pacific and Caribbean tectonic plates.

There are about 200 pyramids in the great city of *Tikal*, including the Temple of the Jaguar, which is 154 feet (47 m) high and dates back to the Maya civilization.

Mayas recorded their history and knowledge on carved stone slabs called *stelae*.

This *jaguar mask* is one of the many masks created by the artisans of Chichicastenango, a city famous for its colorful market.

Belize

The extraordinary *black orchid* is the national flower.

The Maya people did not disappear. Their descendants live in this region in *huts* similar to the traditional ones.

The *Great Blue Hole*, an almost perfect circle, is an ancient cave that collapsed when the sea covered it millions of years ago. Full of marine life, it is 984 feet (300 m) wide and 410 feet (125 m) deep.

Honduras

Volcanoes and a rainbow are part of the country's coat of arms, representing its volcanic mountains and warm, humid climate that brings heavy tropical rains.

Honduras has been producing beautiful *ceramics* since the pre-Columbian era.

The *jaguar* is the largest feline in the Americas and resembles the African leopard, but behaves more like the Asian tiger. For example, the jaguar knows how to swim like an Asian tiger.

One of the tourist attractions in Honduras is swimming with *dolphins*, which live in large numbers in the clear, warm waters.

El Salvador

The *Monument to the Divine Savior of the World* represents Christ's protection over the country. It was rebuilt in 1986 after a serious earthquake.

The *armadillo*, which somewhat resembles an armored tank, digs holes in search of ants and can eat 40,000 in an hour.

Colorful buses transport people throughout the country.

El Salvador attracts tourists who *surf* the powerful waves of the Pacific.

Nicaragua

The magnificently colorful *turquoise-browed motmot*, a symbol of Nicaragua, is one of the few bird species where the females are as beautifully colored as the males.

Until 5,000 years ago the *sloth* used to be much larger, but now this slow forest-dweller is much smaller because it lives on the branches of trees.

A farming community created mysterious rock engravings 4,000 years ago at the foot of *Maderas*, an extinct volcano in the middle of the largest lake in Central America.

Costa Rica

The traditional, *colorful oxcart* of this country used to transport coffee beans and now symbolizes the work, strength, and patience of the Costa Rican people.

The lush forests are home to colorful and often poisonous *frogs*.

Divers from all over the world visit the warm waters of the Caribbean Sea to see the *colorful fish,* turtles, and coral reefs.

The *scarlet macaw*, a beautiful, bright-red parrot, is becoming increasingly rare. It can live for 60 years or more and can mimic human language very well.

Panamá

The *F&F Tower*, 797 feet (243 m) high, an office skyscraper that has garnered much recognition for its beauty and functionality, is the new symbol of Panamá City.

The **Panama Canal**, completed in 1914, is one of the greatest engineering works in history. It is a man-made canal that connects the Pacific and Atlantic oceans.

In local legends, the **giant anteater**, a mammal as big as a large dog, plays the same role as the cunning fox in our own fairy tales.

The wrecks of many **caravels**, a small sailboat, and galleons, a square-rigged ship, sit at the bottom of the Caribbean Sea and are still being explored by treasure seekers.

The rivers of Panama are short and treacherous, and adventurous tourists **raft** their strong rapids.

Sailfish, which race through Panama's waters, are one of the fastest fish in the world.

English and Dutch **pirates** pillaged the South American riches that the Spaniards transported through Panama.

The splendors of ancient cultures of Central America are revealed through **jewels** like this, which belonged to a warrior chief.

Bahamas

The **Atlantis Paradise Island** resort, a complex that includes a mega-hotel with 600 rooms plus a water park and a casino, has been featured in many films.

The Bahamas are a **tourist paradise** made up of hundreds of islands and islets.

One of the biggest tourist attractions in the Bahamas is the **sharks**. Divers encounter many of them, from the shy nurse shark to the more aggressive bull shark.

The two white bell towers of the **Catholic church of Nassau**, built in 1947, guide sailors who are far out to sea.

The juicy local **fruit** like pineapples, grapefruit, and oranges make delicious juices.

Dancers in costumes dance to the rhythm of the **goombay** drum during spectacular masquerades that date back to the era of slavery.

Cuba

One of the symbols of Cuba is the **National Capitol Building**, which resembles the U.S. Capitol. It used to be the seat of the government, but now houses the Cuban Academy of Sciences.

Specialized workers package **Cuban cigars** by hand.

Despite being an American, **Ernest Hemingway**, a great writer and journalist who made his home in Cuba for 20 years, is one of the many symbols of this island and its rich culture.

The same goes for the Argentinian revolutionary **Ernesto Guevara**, called "El Che" (which translates to "hey, you"), who supported socialism, or a system that gave money and support to all people.

In Cuba, there are beautiful **cars from the '50s** that date back to the time of the revolution, when the Cubans weren't allowed to import, or bring new international things, like cars, onto the island.

The **Cuba libre** is a classic drink that represents the fusion between North American culture (Coca-Cola) and Caribbean culture (rum).

The **Cuban tody** is a bright green bird that lives only on this island. While it's hard to see, the tody's singing can be heard easily.

Jamaica

The **Lion of Judah** is the spiritual guide of the Rastafarians, the descendants of slaves brought to Jamaica.

As well as being religious, **Rastafarians**, like Bob Marley, created rhythms such as calypso and reggae, one of the fundamental musical styles of the modern world.

Coconut water is 100 percent natural, sweet, and also very healthy—so much so that it can be used to clean wounds.

The feathers of a Jamaican species of **hummingbird** are much longer than its body, 6 inches (15 cm) versus the typical 3 inches (8 cm).

Haiti

The iron structure at the **Marché en Fer**, Port-au-Prince's famous covered market, was brought to Haiti at the end of the 19th century from Paris and rebuilt after the catastrophic earthquake of 2010.

Baron Samedi, an important voodoo spirit in Haitian culture, leads the dead to the afterlife and is called upon by those seeking strength and protection.

The characteristic **boats of the Haitian fishermen** have triangular sails, similar to those seen in East Africa.

Dominican Republic

The *merengue*, a style of music that has its roots in Caribbean, African, and European cultures, is a popular dance to perform in costume in the Dominican Republic.

The *soursop* is a large fruit that can weigh up to 5.5 pounds (2.5 kg) and is rich in vitamins, sugars, and proteins.

The *green iguana*, a lizard 6 feet (2 m) long, is aggressive, but eats mainly leaves, grass, and flowers.

Puerto Rico

Fort San Cristóbal is the largest Spanish fort in the Americas. In the 18th century it surrounded all of San Juan, the capital of Puerto Rico.

The *coquí frog* is an amphibian from Puerto Rico. Instead of "ribbit," it screams "co-kee."

The *masks* with long horns worn at Puerto Rican festivals like the Ponce Carnival derive from the masks worn by the Taino, the ancient people that inhabited the Caribbean.

Guadeloupe

Hibiscus, a plant with large red or pink flowers, is native to Asia but is Guadeloupe's national flower.

The *traditional dress* for women in Guadeloupe combines French elegance with Caribbean colors.

There is an *underwater statue* of the scientist and filmmaker Jacques Cousteau in the big marine reserve named after him in Guadeloupe.

Dominica

When running water arrived in Dominica, they celebrated by covering an old fountain with an elegant *dome*.

Dominica, like other Caribbean islands, has volcanoes and *hot springs*.

Some of the scenes with *Jack Sparrow* in *Pirates of the Caribbean* were shot in Dominica.

Martinique

The cathedral *Sacré Coeur de Balata* is a replica of Sacré Coeur in Paris, only five times smaller.

In 1902, *Mount Pelée*, a semi-active volcano in Martinique, erupted and buried the town of Saint-Pierre and many of its inhabitants, much like Pompeii in Italy.

Trinidad and Tobago

The Parliament of Trinidad and Tobago meet in the *Red House*, which was painted at the end of the 19th century to celebrate the Jubilee of Queen Victoria of Great Britain.

The *scarlet ibis*, an unmistakable bird, is one of the symbols of Trinidad and Tobago. The chicks are born gray or brown but turn red from eating shrimp, their favorite food.

In Trinidad and Tobago, people wear *masks* and walk on stilts to remember the protective spirits who crossed the ocean on foot to follow the African slaves.

Grenada

The pulpy *papaya* is found in many tropical regions but is native to Central America, where it has been cultivated for centuries.

South America

Atlantic Ocean

BRAZIL

VENEZUELA

* Caracas

GUYANA

* Georgetown

SURINAME

* Paramaribo

FRENCH GUIANA (FR)

* Cayenne

COLOMBIA

* Bogotá

ECUADOR

* Quito

PERÚ

* Lima

* La Paz

Galápagos Islands (ECUADOR)

Puerto Baquerizo Moreno

PARAGUAY

Asunción

URUGUAY

Montevideo

CHILE

Santiago

Buenos Aires

ARGENTINA

Pacific Ocean

Grytviken

South Georgia and the South Sandwich Islands (UK)

Falkland Islands (UK)

Stanley

Link to download the map:

https://www.hachettebookgroup.com/south-america

Central America and South America

From Tropics to Ice Fields

When you look at a globe, South America looks like a fruit suspended from a large branch that is North America, hanging by a stem that is Central America. And if you look closer, you'll see that the east coast of South America interlocks perfectly with Africa's outline.

Polish researcher Alfred Wegener noticed this in 1910 and understood that South America and Africa are two pieces of a giant, dismantled puzzle. In fact, 134 million years ago, the two continents were united as part of the supercontinent Gondwana.

Geology has also confirmed this. South America and Africa have similar rare minerals like gold, diamonds, copper, and uranium.

South America reminds us how North America was formed. It also collided with the Pacific plate, creating mountains and active volcanoes on one side and remaining flat on the other side. There are also big rivers here, like the Amazon River (4,345 mi/6,993 km) and spectacular waterfalls like Iguazú Falls and Angel Falls (3,212 ft/ 979 m high).

Central America rose from the bottom of the ocean 15 million years ago, connecting North America and South America.

From the north of Mexico to Cape Horn in southern Chile, Central America and South America measure 7,300 miles (11,750 km). Because it spans such a long distance, it includes all different types of climates, like very hot summers in Brazil and the cold temperatures in southern Chile and Argentina.

The Andes Mountains are the longest mountain range in the world (4,350 mi/7,000 km). The mountain range is on the west coast of the continent and stretches across seven countries: Venezuela, Colombia, Ecuador, Perú, Bolivia, Chile, and Argentina. The humid Amazon rain forest is to the east of the mountains, and deserts like the Atacama are west of the mountains.

South America is closer to Antarctica than any other continent. The southern tip is home to Los Glaciares National Park, which has 656 glaciers, including the 19-mile (30-km) Perito Moreno.

There are parts of Central and South America that humans have never lived in. They are full of animals like the guanaco (similar to the African camel), the sloth, the giant anteater, and the Amazon river dolphin. There are even animals in forests that have never been discovered.

North and South America are connected by the Isthmus of Panamá. It's a narrow piece of land in the country of Panamá.

Sea life and other species started traveling between the two continents only 2.5 million years ago. Scientists believe humans arrived in South America from North America about 13,000 years ago. The oldest bones found belonged to a woman given the name Luzia, who lived 11,500 years ago in what is now Brazil.

Once they arrived in South America, some people from North America had to adapt to the lack of oxygen in the Andes Mountains and others had to adapt to the hot jungle in the Amazon.

Inhabitants of the deserts—Mexicans, Peruvians, and Chileans—and of the prairies (like gauchos) and the cold Patagonia, were able to prosper in places without many resources. These people have created original, and often very rich, cultures.

South America has a history of many rich cultures like the Olmecs, the Mayas, and the Aztecs in Mexico, the Chavin, Nazca, and Inca civilizations in Perú, and many others.

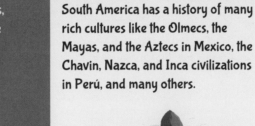

Today, the South American people have a wonderful mix of traditions and a large population that live in big cities like Mexico City in Mexico, São Paulo in Brazil, and Lima in Perú.

There are also smaller cities like Manaus, which is in the middle of the Brazilian jungle. Brasilia, the capital of Brazil, is a very modern city that was built in 1960.

South America has many big outdoor spaces, natural wonders, and resources. Oil, copper, and meat from the Great Plains are important major exports.

South America is active in scientific research and environmental conservation. It's home to the world's second-largest radio telescope in the Arecibo Observatory in Puerto Rico, and to the Galápagos Islands off the coast of Ecuador, which are full of unique wildlife. Tourism is also very important to the continent.

South America

Colombia

 The **Primatial Cathedral of Bogotá** was built in the early 19th century and is one of the largest churches in South America.

 Nevado del Ruiz, 17,717 feet (5,321 m) high, is an active volcano that is very dangerous due to its pyroclastic flow, clouds of gas, and rock that flow from the crater even during small eruptions.

 The **Peñón de Guatapé** is a 10-million-ton (9 million metric tons), nearly 7,005-foot (2,135-m) rock in the town of Guatapé. A staircase was built on the side of the rock and there's even a store at the top of it.

 Many people visit the **Las Lajas Sanctuary**, which began to be built in the 18th century on the spot where some believe a deaf-mute child saw the Virgin Mary.

 Women in colorful costumes sell **tropical fruit** like watermelons, bananas, avocados, and more in the city of Cartagena.

 The **boa constrictor** is 4–13 feet (1–4 m) long and weighs up to 65 pounds (30 kg). It is a dangerous snake that eats its prey's entire body, and it will even eat an **ocelot**, a wild cat that lives in the forest.

 According to a Colombian legend, **emeralds** are the tears of Fura, the first woman in the world that was created by the god Are.

 This magnificent metallic-blue **butterfly** (**Rhetus periander**) is very shy and difficult to see in the wild.

 Kapok trees are also called "cotton trees" because they produce wool-like seeds that can be used to stuff cushions.

Venezuela

 The **Parque Cristal** is a steel building 338 feet (103 m) tall that looks like a crystal cube in the city of Caracas, the capital of Venezuela.

 Angel Falls is the highest uninterrupted waterfall in the world. The water comes from a *tepuí*, a sort of tabletop mountain whose flat top is isolated from the world below by vertical walls.

 The **Venezuelan troupial** is the national bird of Venezuela. It is related to the sparrow but is much bigger and more colorful.

 The **giant vase sculpture in Quibor** is an example of the pottery created by natives in South America before Europeans arrived in the 16th century.

 Some people believe the masks worn by people in the **Corpus Christi festival** represent the demons who once punished the mean and lazy citizens of San Francisco de Yare.

 Venezuela's **oil deposits** are important for the country's economy and have led to its growth.

 Half the population of the Amazon rain forest in the south of Venezuela are **natives** who still follow in part the traditional way of life.

 The red berries of the **coffee** plant are Venezuela's biggest agricultural resource.

 The **keel-billed toucan** has a large, brightly colored beak that looks very heavy, but it is actually spongy and light.

Guyana

 A large clock tower has told the time over the lively **Stabroek Market** in Georgetown since 1881.

 Cricket is a typical English sport and was introduced to Guyana when it was a British colony.

 Diamonds were discovered by chance in 1890 in the forests of Guyana. They are still being mined by searchers today.

 Shrimp and crayfish are fishermen's biggest resources in Guyana.

 Kaieteur Falls is an Amazon waterfall that is 741 feet (226 m) high, but is the largest in the world by the amount of water flowing over it.

 The **margay** is a small leopard that behaves more like a monkey. It lives in the trees and jumps from branch to branch.

Suriname

 The slender **royal palm** is the symbol of Suriname and other South American countries. It is grown all over the world.

 A **frog** with fluorescent, lavender-colored spots was discovered in Suriname in 2006.

 Guianan cock-of-the-rock male birds have bright orange feathers and dance to attract females.

The colorful birds of Suriname provide beautiful multicolored feathers that are used to make **tribal headdresses**.

French Guiana

Space missions of French and European space agencies (ESA) are launched from the **Centre Spatial Guyanais.**

The full name of this monkey commonly called **saki** is "white-faced saki" because of the male's light-colored beard.

Leatherback sea turtles lay their eggs on the beach of Awala-Yalimapo.

Ecuador

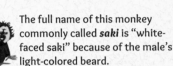
Building work began on the **Basilica of the National Vow** more than 120 years ago, but it has not yet been completed, because according to legend, finishing the building would lead to the end of the world.

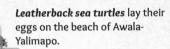
Panama hats, the most famous straw hats in the world, are made in Ecuador, not Panamá. They are so thin that they can be rolled up like cigars.

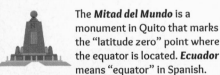
The **Mitad del Mundo** is a monument in Quito that marks the "latitude zero" point where the equator is located. **Ecuador** means "equator" in Spanish.

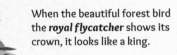
When the beautiful forest bird the **royal flycatcher** shows its crown, it looks like a king.

Galápagos Islands

The English naturalist **Charles Darwin** found important evidence of the evolution of species when he traveled to this untouched group of islands in 1835.

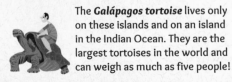
The **Galápagos tortoise** lives only on these islands and on an island in the Indian Ocean. They are the largest tortoises in the world and can weigh as much as five people!

The **marine iguana** is found only on the Galápagos. It's a strong swimmer and hunts in the sea.

Perú

Ancient Peruvians thanked the Sun at the end of the potato and corn harvest by sacrificing a black llama using a **tumi**, a knife with a half-moon blade.

The Andes have many active volcanoes, but **Huascarán**, Perú's highest peak (22,205 ft/6,768 m), is made of solid rock.

Machu Picchu was a city of the Inca empire that was built in the Andes Mountains more than 500 years ago. Its ruins are the most popular tourist attraction in Perú.

Peruvians have created these incredible **terraced crop fields** on the steep sides of the mountains for centuries.

Andean condors are one of the largest birds in the world that can fly. The strong winds from the Andes Mountains let them glide through the air without flapping their wings.

In Perú, the art of weaving is over 5,000 years old. Wool from alpacas, which are relatives of llamas and camels, are used to make the **colorful clothes** worn by the Andean people.

The **Nazca lines** are drawings called geoglyphs, lines etched into the sands of the Nazca desert at least 1,500 years ago. Some are hundreds of feet long and can only be seen from airplanes.

The Uros people lived on the shores of Lake Titicaca and used marsh reeds to build **canoes** and artificial floating islands for their huts.

The **blue-footed booby** is a seabird that dives into the water to catch fish. Its blue legs help the males to impress the females.

Bolivia

The **Gate of the Sun** is a gate carved out of a single block of stone that is located in Tiwanaku. It is a large religious center that was abandoned 1,000 years ago.

The **University of Saint Francis Xavier** in Sucre, Bolivia, was founded 400 years ago and is the second-oldest university in the Americas.

Bolivian **farmers** have been growing potatoes for 10,000 years.

There is a simple and beautiful 17th-century **mud brick church** in the middle of the mountains of Sajama National Park.

There were large salt lakes in southwest Bolivia 40,000 years ago. When the water dried up, they left behind layers of salt known as **salt deserts**.

The Salar de Uyuni is the largest natural salt flat in the world, and salt-loving **flamingos** lay their eggs here.

The **avocado** is a fruit native to Central America, but it grows in all hot and humid climates, like in eastern Bolivia, where the Amazon rain forest begins.

Brazil

The Warriors statue can be found in the Three Powers Plaza in the capital city of Brasilia.

The pineapple is native to South America. Some varieties, like the **red pineapple**, can't be eaten but are used as ornamental plants.

Coffee comes from Africa, but in Brazil it found the perfect soil. The coffee produced here is some of the best in the world.

The Amazon forest still protects native populations like the **Yanomami**, descendants of the first humans who arrived here 10,000 years ago.

The **Amazon rain forest** is the world's largest tropical rain forest. Its trees create 20 percent of the world's oxygen.

The **Amazon Theatre** was built in the late 19th century in the city of Manaus, which is in the middle of the forest.

The most famous fish of the Amazon is the *piranha*. They have sharp teeth but rarely attack people.

 Pink dolphins live thousands of miles from the sea in the rivers and lakes of the Amazon.

 The rivers of Brazil are the oldest and largest roads in the country. They are crossed by *riverboats* and carry both goods and passengers.

 The *marmoset* is a small monkey with tufts of white fur close to its ears. It lives high up in rainforest trees, where it hunts for insects and eats tree sap.

 Anacondas are the largest snakes in the world. They can grow up to 30 feet (9 m) long and weigh up to 550 pounds (250 kg).

 The *capybara* is the largest rodent in the world. It's the size of a large dog, loves water and sometimes even sleeps there, and is a very good swimmer.

 Moqueca is a spicy Brazilian fish stew. It's named after the wooden grill on which the meat and fish are dried.

 Capoeira is a spectacular martial art that was possibly invented by Africans fleeing slavery. It is very similar to a dance.

 São Paulo is home to 20 million people, making it the largest city in the world where Portuguese is spoken.

 Brazil has won the *FIFA World Cup*, the most important soccer tournament in the world, five times, more than any other country.

 Edson Arantes do Nascimento, known by his nickname *Pelé*, was a Brazilian soccer player from 1957 to 1971. He is considered the greatest soccer player of all time.

 The *Christ the Redeemer* statue in Rio de Janeiro is considered one of the seven wonders of the modern world.

 Brazilian restaurants often serve food on *skewers,* or sticks, a practice that comes from the cuisine of the natives and the gauchos (cowboys), who cooked large pieces of meat on a spit planted in the fire.

 Agate is a quartz mineral of volcanic origin with wonderful colors and patterns that is found in Brazil in very large rock formations called geodes.

 The people of Mato Grosso wear wonderful *feather headdresses* on special occasions.

 The long stretches of sand in the state of Santa Catarina are perfect for beach sports like *volleyball*.

 The *toco toucan* is the largest species of toucan and does not like the forest. It is mostly found in areas with the fewest trees, like the savanna or open clearings.

 The *Iguazú Falls* includes 275 individual waterfalls over 2 miles (3 km). The falls are divided between Brazil and Argentina and are among the most spectacular in the world.

 Lençóis Maranhenses National Park can look like a desert but it actually receives a lot of rain, which forms its blue and green lakes.

 Samba is a lively, fast, and popular Brazilian dance that originated in the 1920s. Female samba dancers sometimes wear costumes full of jewels and feathers for parades and festivals.

Uruguay

 The *Legislative Palace* is a government building in the capital city of Montevideo. It was designed by an Italian architect who was inspired by the classical architecture of Greece and Rome.

 The *candombe* is drum music and dance that comes from African slaves.

 La Mano is a gigantic sculpture created on the beach of Punta del Este by Mario Irarrázabal in 1982. It is one of the most famous monuments in Uruguay.

Paraguay

 Paraguay's national bird is the *bare-throated bellbird*. It has a sharp, metallic voice that sometimes sounds like a dentist's drill.

 The *Guaraní* are a native people of Paraguay that consider themselves to be the responsible guardians of nature.

 Ñandutí is a traditional Paraguayan lace of Spanish origin that is as fine as a spider web.

 The *chipa* is a small cheese bread that is sometimes shaped as a donut. It has been made by the Guaraní for centuries and is a classic snack in Paraguay.

Argentina

 The tango dance and the colored houses (originally painted with paint left over from ships) are the main attractions of *La Boca*, the most visited district of Buenos Aires.

 The *Argentina national football team* is one of the best in the world.

 Asado is an Argentinian way of grilling meat. Large cuts of beef, sheep, or goat are cooked over a low heat.

Gauchos are cowboys from the pampas, or the plains, of Argentina, Chile, and Uruguay.

 Maté is a traditional drink in Argentina that's similar to tea or coffee.

 The **heliconia plant** has big leaves that certain bats use as shelter and flowers that hummingbirds eat.

 The **Tren a las Nubes**, or Train to the Clouds, in the city of Salta takes tourists from a low of 3,280 feet (1,000 m) above sea level up to a high of 13,845 feet (4,220 m), so it really does seem like it's heading for the clouds.

 The **vicuña** is related to the llama, but is much more delicate and timid.

 The **tango** is a very famous dance that has spread across the whole world. It was born in Argentina during the musical gatherings of African slaves, called **tambo** or **tango**.

 The rivers and fairy-tale lakes of the Andes are perfect for water sports such as **kayaking** and rafting.

 Argentina is the largest **wine** producer in South America and the sixth-largest in the world.

 A **poncho** is a traditional piece of clothing that is worn to protect against the cold and rain. In Argentina, each region has a poncho with its own particular colors.

 Argentina has been farming **cattle** for more than 500 years. Spanish settlers brought them to the country in 1536.

 German-style **beer** is drunk in the town of Bariloche, which is in the Andes. The town was settled by German-speaking immigrants in the 19th century.

 The **rhea** is a big bird from the Argentinian plains that, at 55 pounds (25 kg), is too heavy to fly but runs very fast, like the ostrich and the Australian emu.

 The **Perito Moreno glacier** is three miles long and rises 240 feet (73 m) above the blue waters of Argentino Lake.

 Cerro Torre is an extraordinary mountain in Patagonia. It's one of the most beautiful in the world and one of the most difficult to climb.

 Magellanic penguins live in very big colonies. They were named after the Portuguese explorer Ferdinand Magellan.

 The **elephant seal** is a giant seal with a trunk that weighs up to 6,000 pounds.

 The **southern right whale** swims north in winter and swims south toward Antarctica in summer.

 Portuguese explorer Ferdinand Magellan used a **carrack**, a large sailing ship, when he sailed around the world in the 16th century.

Chile

 Cerro de los Siete Colores (Hill of Seven Colors) is called the "mountain of the seven skirts" by the locals because its different colors look like the skirts of the traditional costumes.

 The **Gran Torre Santiago** is a 984-foot (300-m) skyscraper that opened in 2014 in the capital city of Santiago.

 The Chilean sculptor Mario Irarrázabal created a sculpture called the **Hand of the Desert** that rises up from the sand in the Atacama Desert in Chile.

 The **Atacama Desert** may be the oldest in the world and driest desert in the world. It hasn't rained in some areas for centuries.

 Guanacos are in the camel family and are related to llamas, alpacas, and vicuñas.

 The Chilean bellflower is called **copihue**, meaning "upside down."

 The **Villarrica volcano** is one of the most active in Chile and contains a lava lake. The volcano has erupted 65 times in less than 500 years.

 The granite mountains of southern Chile are vertical and sharp, making them difficult for even the best of **climbers**.

Falkland Islands

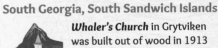 The Falkland Islands are a British territory and has **double-decker buses** like the ones in London.

 The **southern rockhopper penguin** has long yellow feathers on the sides of its head that look like eyebrows.

South Georgia, South Sandwich Islands

 Whaler's Church in Grytviken was built out of wood in 1913 by the whalers who founded the settlement.

Link to download the map:

https://www.hachettebookgroup.com/oceania

Bonin Islands
(JAPAN)

Wake Islands (US)

Northern Mariana Islands (US)

Guam (US)

MARSHALL ISLANDS

FEDERATED STATES OF MICRONESIA

PALAU

NAURU

TUVA

PAPUA NEW GUINEA

SOLOMON ISLANDS

Gulf of Carpentaria

Coral Sea

VANUATU

Coral Sea Islands
(AUS)

New Caledonia
(FRANCE)

AUSTRALIA

Norfolk Island (Aus)

Great Australian Bight

Tasman Sea

Inhabitants:
40 million

Surface area:
3.3 million square miles (8.5 million km^2)

NEW ZEALAND

Midway Atoll (US)

Hawaii (US)

Johnston Atoll (US)

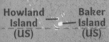

Kingman Reef (US) ——— Palmyra Atoll (US)

Howland Island (US) ——— Baker Island (US)

Jarvis Island (US)

KIRIBATI

Pacific Ocean

Tokelau (NZ)

Easter Island (CHILE)

Juan Fernández Islands (CHILE)

Wallis and Futuna (FR)   SAMOA

American Samoa (US)

TONGA

Niue (NZ)

COOK ISLANDS

FIJI

French Polynesia (FR)

Pitcairn Islands (UK)

Oceania

Oceania
The Kingdom of the Sea

Australia is the world's smallest continent. It was first formed 4.4 billion years ago, back when the moon was still forming!

Australia doesn't have high mountains—it's the flattest of all the continents. It is home to enormous rock formations like Uluru and Kata Tjuta in the center of the continent.

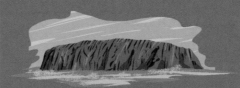

Australia contains a desert that is bigger than all of Europe, but it also has lush forest lands on the southeastern coast. Even though it's very dry, Australia has many rivers, the longest of which is the Murray River, which runs for 1,550 miles (2,500 km). Its typical tree is the eucalyptus, which can grow 330 feet (100 m) tall.

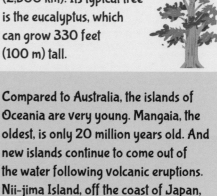

Australia's wildlife includes the platypus, an extraordinary mammal that lays eggs; the kangaroo and the koala, whose babies grow in a pouch on their mothers' bellies; and the emu, a relative of the African ostrich that can be up to 6.5 feet (2 m) high. The kiwi, a bird with very small wings that can't fly, lives in the neighboring island country of New Zealand.

Oceania isn't exactly a piece of land but is composed of 30,000 islands in the Pacific Ocean. Some are big like Papua New Guinea and some are tiny like Nauru, which is less than 3 miles (5 km) long.

Compared to Australia, the islands of Oceania are very young. Mangaia, the oldest, is only 20 million years old. And new islands continue to come out of the water following volcanic eruptions. Nii-jima Island, off the coast of Japan, appeared in 2013 and hasn't yet stopped growing.

The islands of Oceania are almost always linked to volcanoes. Some islands, like New Zealand, were formed from emerged parts of mountain chains. Oceanic islands are formed from isolated volcanoes or atolls, made of coral that grew on the top of flooded volcanoes.

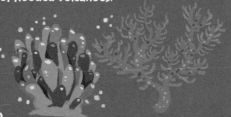

Oceania is full of animals like whales and sea birds that travel for thousands of miles, crabs and sharks that live deep down in the seas, and the colorful creatures of the coral reefs.

The islands of Oceania are in the Earth's tropical zone. Much of the land is covered in thick plants and trees along the coasts and in jungles.

Humans took a long time to explore Oceania. The original inhabitants of Australia are the Aboriginal people who arrived more than 45,000 years ago. They explored the surrounding areas little by little by crossing the ocean, finally reaching New Zealand, which was discovered by the Maori people only 800 years ago.

Oceania's populations came from different places. Australian Aborigines probably arrived from Africa, traveling the entire southern coast of Asia to Indonesia and then crossing the sea on rafts.

The ancestors of the Polynesians may have come from the south of China on double-hulled canoes that could hold entire tribes and their animals across thousands of miles of ocean.

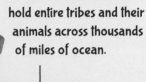

There are 27 nations and 30,000 islands in Oceania. The biggest nations are Australia, Papua New Guinea, and New Zealand. The other islands are much smaller. Tonga is the only nation that is still ruled by an independent king.

Australia has a large economy thanks to natural resources like coal, copper, uranium, diamonds, oil, and natural gases. A lot of farming is done on the large open spaces in the continent.

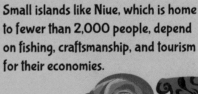

Small islands like Niue, which is home to fewer than 2,000 people, depend on fishing, craftsmanship, and tourism for their economies.

Ancient traditions are still alive in Australia and Oceania. The Australian Aborigines carry out long, ritualistic journeys on foot that they call "walkabouts." On the Pacific Islands, the descendants of the Polynesian warrior people still challenge each other to arm wrestling matches and are very good at rugby.

Singing, dancing, and tattoos are important parts of all of Oceania's cultures. They are closely tied with religion. The people of the continent didn't leave behind many monuments, but the ones that they did, like the mysterious *moai* on Easter Island, are extraordinary.

With its seas, Oceania is bigger than all the other continents put together, but only has 40 million people living there. That's about the population of the state of California. More than half the people live in big cities like Sydney, which is home to 5 million people.

PAPUA NEW GUINEA

★ Port Moresby

Torres Straits

Gulf of Carpentaria

AUSTRALIA

Sydney

Canberra

Great Australian Bight

Tasmania (AUS)

Hobart

100m

Hobart

Australia, Papua New Guinea, and New Zealand

Coral Sea

Pacific Ocean

Tasman Sea

Wellington ✪

NEW ZEALAND

Bonin Islands (JAPAN)

Midway Atoll (US)

Northern
Mariana
Islands (US)

Mariana Trench

Saipan ✪

Hagåtña ✪ Guam (US)

Wake Island (us)

MARSHALL ISLANDS

PALAU

Ngerulmud ✪

FEDERATED STATES OF MICRONESIA

Palikir ✪

Majuro ✪

Howland
Island (us)

Baker Island
(us)

South
Tarawa ✪

Yaren ✪

NAURU

KIRIBA

SOLOMON ISLANDS

TUVALU

Vaiaku ✪

Honiara ✪

VANUATU

Mata-Ut

Wallis and Futuna
(FR)

Coral Sea Islands
(AUS)

New Caledonia
(FR)

Port Vila ✪

Suva ✪

FIJI

Nouméa ✪

Nuku'al

Link to download the map:

https://www.hachettebookgroup.com/the-pacific-islands

Norfolk Island (AUS)

The Pacific Islands

Hawaii (US)

Honolulu ✦

Johnston Atoll (us)

Kingman Reef (us) — Palmyra Atoll (us)

Pacific Ocean

Jarvis Island (us)

Tokelau (NZ)

Nukunonu ✦

American Samoa (us)

SAMOA
Apia

Pago Pago

COOK ISLANDS

$2

Niue (NZ)

Alofi ✦

TONGA

Avarua ✦

Papeete ✦

French Polynesia

Hanga Roa

Easter Island (CHILE)

Juan Fernández Islands (CHILE)

San Juan Bautista

Pitcairn Islands (UK)

Adamstown ✦

Oceania
Australia, Papua New Guinea, and New Zealand

Australia

The **Canberra Parliament House** has two wings shaped like boomerangs and a 266-foot (81-m) flagpole.

The **saltwater crocodile** is the largest living reptile. It can be up to 23 feet (7 m) in length and can weigh more than 2,000 pounds (900 kg).

The **Indian Pacific train** follows a railway across the country from Sydney to Perth that is 2,704 miles (4,352 km) long. It takes 2 days and 17 hours to get from the east coast to the west coast.

The Canberra Balloon Spectacular is one of the four most famous **hot air balloon** shows in the world.

Boomerangs were originally created by the Aborigines, the native people of Australia. They were once used in hunting and war and today they are used for sport.

"Mad" Max is one of the most beloved movie heroes of the country. His adventures were set in Australia.

Snowboarding is practiced on the Australian slopes of Mount Hotham and Mount Buffalo.

The **Flying Doctor** is an air ambulance service that treats and rescues people in the most isolated areas of Australia.

Ayers Rock is the largest rock mass of the Australian Outback, which is what the large, open area in the middle of the country is called. The rock is a sacred site for the Aboriginal people, who call it Uluru.

The **Sydney Opera House** is one of the most significant works of architecture of the 20th century and is a true icon of Australia.

The **emu** is the second largest bird in the world. The ostrich is the largest. Emus, like ostriches, cannot fly because they are so big.

The **red kangaroo** lives all over Australia. It is the largest living marsupial on Earth. Marsupials are animals that keep their babies in pouches after they are born.

The **koala** is only active for two hours a day and feeds on eucalyptus leaves, which provide it with all the fluids it needs.

A third of the world's diamond production comes from the Kimberley region of Australia.

Arabian camels were brought to Australia some years ago to help carry things in the dry climate.

The **Great Barrier Reef** is over 1,400 miles (2,300 km) long and is the largest reef in the world.

The **didgeridoo** is an ancient aboriginal wind instrument made of wood that creates a deep and vibrant sound.

The **black widow** lives in Australia. It is quite small but is one of the most poisonous spiders in the world.

Rodeo is a very popular sport in Australia that was first brought to the country in the 1880s.

The **merino sheep** is kept for its fine, valuable wool. Half of the world's merino wool production comes from Australia.

The **platypus** is a very unique mammal because it lays eggs, which is something that birds and fish do. The Aborigines call it **boondaburra**.

The **Devils Marbles** rock spheres look like islands in the desert. They were created by erosion over millions of years.

Kalgoorlie is a city in Western Australia famous for its Super Pit, a vast, open-air **gold mine**.

Australia began making **wine** around 200 years ago. There are about 2,400 wineries in the 65 wine regions around the country.

The Australian Grand Prix has been part of the **Formula One** car racing world championship since 1985.

You can see a **penguin** parade at sunset on Phillip Island. Every evening, little penguins come out of the ocean to spend the night in their sand burrows, or holes, on the beach.

Tasmania

The **Tasmanian devil** is a marsupial that only lives on the island of Tasmania. They may look like little bears, but they have very sharp teeth and are very aggressive.

The **Eucalyptus regnans** is a kind of tall eucalyptus tree that grows in southeastern Australia and Tasmania.

New Zealand (North Island)

The **Wellington cable cars** are a symbol of the city and one of its main tourist attractions.

The **Maori** people arrived from Polynesia between AD 1250 and 1300. They used small canoes to fish and sail on the rivers, and large canoes for war and ocean crossings.

The **haka** is a traditional dance of the Maori people, made famous by the All Blacks, New Zealand's national rugby union team.

The Maori are masters of wood carving. They carve decorations onto canoes, houses, and **masks**, using the same symbols they tattoo on their bodies.

New Zealand (South Island)

The **lobster** industry is the most thriving business in the town of Kaikoura, whose name in Maori means "lobster eaters."

Aoraki/Mount Cook is 12,218 feet (3,724 m), making it the highest mountain in New Zealand.

The **hei-tiki** is the typical Maori ornament, usually made of jade, a green stone. They are often handed down from one generation to the next.

The **takahē** is a native, flightless bird of New Zealand.

Papua New Guinea

Whale watching is a popular tourist activity in this country.

Ulawun is located on the island of New Britain in Papua New Guinea and is one of the most dangerous volcanoes in the world.

The **outrigger canoe** is a typical canoe of Oceania but may have been created in Southeast Asia.

Three-quarters of the land in Papua New Guinea is covered in **tropical rain forest**.

Hundreds of **indigenous** ethnic groups live in Papua New Guinea.

Indigenous people with colorful faces and incredible headdresses compete in dance, singing, and beauty contests during the **sing-sing**, the great gathering of the tribes of Papua New Guinea.

The Pacific Islands

Palau

The **Airai Bai** is a traditional meetinghouse on Babeldaob, the largest island in Palau.

Micronesia

Tattoos are used as symbols of the different tribes of Oceania.

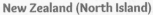
The strong ocean waves and warm waters of Micronesia make these islands perfect for **surfing**.

Northern Mariana Islands

The **proa boats** of the Mariana Islands have two sails, making them very fast and easy to control.

Bonin Islands

The Bonin Islands or Ogasawara are islands belonging to **Japan** and are part of the city of Tokyo, which is 600 miles (1,000 km) to the north.

Marshall Islands

The **pandanus fruit** is very common on the Marshall Islands. It has a similar shape to the pineapple.

In 2011 the Marshall Islands became the largest **shark** sanctuary in the world.

Nauru

The peaceful people of Nauru transformed into warriors after the arrival of the Europeans. Some wore armor made of **plant fibers**.

Solomon Islands

The **thamakau** is the traditional canoe of the Solomon Islands. They are light and decorated and were once used for war.

Coral Sea Islands

Shipwrecks from World War II's **Battle of the Coral Sea** between Japan and the United States lie at the bottom of the Coral Sea.

Tuvalu

Kaleve is a palm wine made in Tuvalu that is drunk under different names throughout Oceania.

Wallis and Futuna

The population of this small group of islands are mostly farmers and pick **coconuts**.

Vanuatu

Vanuatu's **rambaramps** were statues that featured the skulls of important ancestors and depicted their spirit.

For centuries, the men of Vanuatu have practiced **land-diving**, which is similar to bungee jumping. It's a ritual where men jump from a height of 100 feet (30 m) with their ankles tied to two vines.

New Caledonia

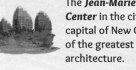

The **Jean-Marie Tjibaou Cultural Center** in the city of Nouméa, the capital of New Caledonia, is one of the greatest works of modern architecture.

Fiji

The **tagimaucia flower** is the national flower of these islands and blooms between the end of September and the end of December.

Rugby is the national sport of Fiji, which has one of the best teams in the world.

The **haka dance** is a traditional war dance that is now sometimes performed before rugby matches by the Oceania teams.

The **mahi-mahi** is a very common fish in Fiji. It grows quickly and eats a lot.

The **meke** is a traditional dance in Fiji performed by both men and women.

Sea snakes are one of the most poisonous reptiles on the Earth but only bite when they feel that they are in danger.

The **flying fox** that lives on these islands is actually a bat.

Only the male **orange fruit doves** of Fiji have bright orange feathers. The females are a dark green color.

Tonga

The **Royal Order of the Crown of Tonga** is a group of knights founded in 1913.

The ancient inhabitants of Tonga were great and powerful **warriors**.

Humpback whales cross through the waters of Tonga. They are identifiable by their white belly and fins.

The **wild pig** usually lives in the forest, but some in Tonga go to the sea to eat fish in the shallow water.

Samoa

Tagaloa is a mythical figure in Samoa. He is a king, the creator of the universe, and the head of the gods of Samoa. He crosses the sea using the islands as if they were a bridge.

Starfish live in seas all over the world, but the most colorful ones are found in tropical seas like this one.

Tokelau

The **sailfish** has a long fin on its back that looks like a sail and can be up to 5 feet (1.5 m) tall.

Guests receive beautiful **crowns of fragrant flowers** on the islands of Oceania that can also be made of fruit, leaves, ferns, walnuts, and shells.

American Samoa

The main industry in American Samoa is **canned tuna**, which is exported primarily to the United States.

In the Samoan **fire dance**, the dancer moves to the rhythm of the drums with a lighted torch.

Kiribati

The **great frigatebird** can fly for more than a week without resting. It is featured on the flag of Kiribati.

Copra is a dried coconut meat that is used for oils and creams.

Bread trees on the island of Kiribati grow fruit called breadfruit that is rich in carbohydrates and can be baked just like bread.

The **wahoo** is a fast tropical water fish that shaped like a torpedo.

Humpback whales swim for the warm waters of central Oceania in winter with their newborn babies.

The **spotted dolphin** looks like the common dolphin but can do backward somersaults and other tricks.

Niue

Rugby is the most popular sport in Niue, which also has a **female team**.

Cook Islands

The **tiaré flower** is the national flower of the Cook Islands. Men and women wear the flowers during special ceremonies and holidays

Cook Islands' **black pearls** are many different shades of black because they are formed inside grayish-black oyster shells.

Here and on other islands of Oceania, the **conch** shell is played to announce events and to welcome or say goodbye to people.

 The coins used on the Cook Islands have a unique shape, like the **triangular two-dollar coin.**

 The islands are named after Captain **James Cook**, who explored most of Oceania in the 1770s.

 The **giant clams** of the coral reefs produce very large, bright pearls. The largest ever found weighed 14 pounds (6.4 kg).

Hawaii

 Kamehameha I was the first king of the Kingdom of Hawaii from 1782 to 1819. His statue in the center of the capital, Honolulu, is covered in gold.

 Kū, the god of war, is covered in red feathers, like many of the gods in Hawaiian mythology.

 Mauna Loa is the world's largest active volcano. It has been active for 700,000 years or more.

 The **ukulele** is a typical Hawaiian musical instrument and looks like a small guitar.

 The **reef triggerfish** that lives in the waters of Hawaii is very colorful, but this color fades when it sleeps.

 A white museum was built above the remains of the **USS Arizona** battleship, which has been lying at the bottom of the Pearl Harbor port since December 7, 1941.

French Polynesia

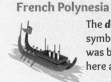 The **double-hulled canoe** is a symbol of French Polynesia that was brought by the first settlers here about 2,000 years ago.

 The typical house in Oceania is a **hut** that is open on the sides and covered with palm leaves.

 The island of **Ua Pou** is in the Marquesas archipelago, which is part of French Polynesia. It is full of strangely shaped, pointed mountains.

 Sometimes ships similar to the fast **clipper ships** from the 19th century are now used for cruises around the islands of French Polynesia.

 The **red ginger** opens its showy flowers in the warm, humid climate of Oceania. It's grown all over the world but rarely blooms elsewhere.

 If it were real, the Mysterious Island, the secret port of the **Nautilus**, a submarine in the famous novel *Twenty Thousand Leagues under the Sea* by French writer Jules Verne, would probably be located somewhere south of French Polynesia.

 The French painter **Paul Gauguin** (1848–1903) traveled to Polynesia for inspiration and ended up spending most of his life there.

 Portrayals of the gods, like this **two-headed idol of Tahiti**, were the most important objects in ancient Polynesian societies.

 Most of the **sea turtles** of French Polynesia are protected, but the green sea turtle is hunted for meat.

If you only count those that live in the **coral reefs**, French Polynesia has more than 900 species of fish, each with its own flamboyant colors.

 The **manta ray** is a unique fish that turns its fins into wings, using them to "fly" through the water.

Midway Atoll

 The Battle of Midway was an important battle that was fought in these waters in 1942, during World War II.

Pitcairn Islands

 In 1789, some people from the sailing ship the **HMS Bounty** landed on the remote Pitcairn Islands after the most famous mutiny in history. A mutiny is when sailors overthrow a ship's captain.

Easter Island

 Moai are stone statues that look like large heads. Researchers believe they were made by Polynesians 1,000 years ago.

 Norwegian explorer Thor Heyerdahl sailed from South America to Polynesia in 1947 on the **Kon-Tiki** raft.

 The waters near Easter Island are home to only a few species of fish, but some, like the **halfbarred wrasse**, have beautiful colors.

Juan Fernández Islands

 Hummingbirds are very common on the Juan Fernández Islands. They are very small and can fly backward.

 The famous book **Robinson Crusoe** by Daniel Defoe may have been inspired by a Scottish sailor who was stranded on these islands 300 years ago.

 Magellanic penguins lay eggs on one of the Juan Fernández Islands.

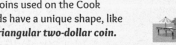

ALASKA

Beaufort Sea

CANADA

Hudson Bay

Baffin Bay

SAVE THE ARCTIC!

Greenland
(DENMARK)

Atlantic Ocean

The Arctic

Bering Strait

Laptev Sea

Arctic Ocean

NORTH POLE

✦ North Pole

NORGE

Kara Sea

RUSSIA

Barents Sea

NORWAY

SWEDEN

FINLAND

Greenland Sea

Inhabitants:
4 million

Surface area:
5.4 million square miles (14 million km²)

Link to download the map:
https://www.hachettebookgroup.com/the-arctic

The Arctic
At the Top of the World

The Arctic isn't a continent, but a sea at the top of the world. It looks like it has land because the sea is covered in ice.

In the Arctic, the sun doesn't set for three months, but for another three months it never rises and it just gets colder and colder.

There is a chain of submerged volcanoes and a massive mountain range below the ice in the Arctic.

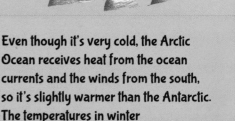

The Arctic changes size depending on the temperature. The thinner ice in the sea melts in the months when there is light (summer) and freezes again in the months when it's dark (winter). Between summer and winter, the ice sheet doubles in size.

The North Pole is in the middle of the Arctic. It is the northern part of the Earth's axis. The axis is an imaginary line through the center of Earth, around which the planet rotates.

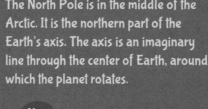

Even though it's very cold, the Arctic Ocean receives heat from the ocean currents and the winds from the south, so it's slightly warmer than the Antarctic. The temperatures in winter don't drop any lower than –58°F (–50°C), while in the summer they can to rise to 50°F (10°C) and above.

–50

The Arctic is full of wildlife including polar bears, seals, whales, and numerous marine birds that live with humans, who began to settling the area 8,000 years ago. The northernmost archeological site in the world is on the north end of Greenland.

The Arctic began to attract explorers in the Middle Ages (AD 500–1500), both for its fascinating mysteriousness and, later, for its natural resources like oil.

Various explorers claimed to have conquered the North Pole, but none of them could prove it until 1926, when Norwegian Roald Amundsen crossed it on board the airship *Norge*.

NORGE

Arctic

 The **North Pole** is the northernmost place on Earth. If you stand there, the only way you can go is south.

 The people living on the arctic ice pack **make a hole in the ice** to fish.

 American explorer **Richard E. Byrd** may have been the first person to fly over the North Pole in 1926. Historians aren't sure if he really did reach the North Pole.

 Ice Camp Barneo is a Russian-run station mostly used for tourists. It needs to be rebuilt every year because the arctic ice is always moving.

 Igloos are made of ice, but body heat warms the inside quickly and it can even get as warm as 60°F (16°C).

 The **Terra Bus** is a special bus with large tires that can transport up to 56 people over ice in the Arctic.

 The **Global Seed Vault** on the island of Spitsbergen is a bank that holds the seeds of most important edible plants for humans.

 The **lion's mane jellyfish** that lives in the cold waters of the Arctic is gigantic. Its tentacles can be 30 feet (10 m) long, but aren't very dangerous.

 In 1926, the **Norge airship** captained by Umberto Nobile flew over the North Pole, three days after Richard Byrd's plane.

 Qalupalik is the imaginary monster that lives in the waters of the Arctic.

 The **arctic fox** can live in very cold temperatures (down to −94°F/−70°C) because its small size means it loses less heat.

 About 13 percent of the undiscovered **oil** in the world is in the Arctic. Scientists warn that removing it could seriously harm the animals and the environment.

 Ecologists study the relationship between people and the environment. Ecologists in the Arctic study global warming, which is causing the polar ice cap to melt.

 The **arctic fulmar** is a seabird that flies south to places like Iceland in the summer to lay eggs and in winter it goes north to the Arctic Ocean.

 Icebergs are pieces of ice that break off glaciers. They're smaller in the Arctic than in Antarctica, although some are as big as buildings.

 Polar bears have a 4-inch (10-cm) layer of fat under their skin to help them keep warm.

 The **walrus** lives along the Arctic Ocean coastline. It's not a great diver, but it can sleep in the water.

 The **beluga whale** is born gray and becomes more and more white as it ages. It lives in very large groups in the waters of the Arctic.

 In 1958, the **USS Nautilus** submarine was the first to cross the entire Arctic Ocean, passing beneath the ice and reaching the North Pole.

 Scientists put trackers on species like the **spotted seal** to observe their movements.

 The **northern lights** are a natural light display where the sky turns shades of green, pink, yellow, and orange.

 In the 19th century, many **sailing ships** became trapped by ice as they explored the Arctic.

 Sleds and **snowshoes** are still used for transportation in the Arctic, but they are a little more modern than they were 5,000 years ago.

 The Earth is tilted on its side so the Arctic is always facing the sun during the summer. The sun never sets and is known as a **midnight sun.**

Atlantic Ocean

Weddell Sea

Norway

Bellingshausen
Sea

United Kingdom

Argentina

SOUTH POLE

Chile

South Pole

Amundsen Sea

Inhabitants:

no information available

Surface area:

5.4 million square miles (4 million km²)

Ross Sea

Antarctica

Pacific Ocean

Australia

Indian Ocean

New Zealand

Australia

France

Link to download the map:

https://www.hachettebookgroup.com/antarctica

Antarctica
The Ice Continent

The rocky crust that forms Antarctica is ancient and formed by numerous upheavals. This is a lonely and different continent.

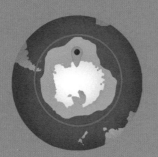

When it was part of the supercontinent Gondwana, Antarctica had a tropical environment and in certain periods even a desert one until 160 million years ago when the other continents began to move away, isolating it farther toward the planet's South Pole.

The process was completed 16 million years ago when the Antarctic Peninsula broke away from the Andean mountain chain and the continent became completely surrounded by the cold ocean currents, transforming it into an ice kingdom.

The marine life, the dinosaurs, and the forests of Antarctica disappeared beneath layers of ice that today are 2.5 miles (4 km) thick. This abundance of life left its traces in the coal deposits that are the main natural resource of the continent along with gas and oil.

The Antarctic is covered in the biggest mass of ice on the planet. The antarctic ice sheet contains 70 percent of all the fresh water in the world. It is also the highest continent in the world. This is one of the reasons why it's colder than the Arctic, with a world record of –128.5°F (–89°C).

−89.2

The continent is divided in two by the Transantarctic Mountains, which are 2,200 miles (3,500 km) long (three times the length of the European Alps) and contain a big, active volcano, Mount Erebus, at 12,448 feet (3,794 m). The McMurdo Dry Valleys, one of only ice-free zones in Antarctica, include the Onyx River. At 20 miles (32 km) long, it is the longest river in Antarctica.

The continent is surrounded by several islands, most of them uninhabited. Villa Las Estrellas is a small town and research center on King George Island. It has 150 inhabitants in summer and 80 in winter.

Even though it isn't the luscious land it once was, Antarctica is home to animals like sea elephants, seals, penguins, and shellfish, along with creatures like tardigrades, also known as water bears. They are microscopic water dwellers that are capable of surviving in harsh conditions much worse than those of the Antarctic.

Antarctica was the last continent to see the arrival of humans. First sighted in 1820 by the Russian ship *Vostok*, it was not reached until 1895, and the South Pole was "conquered" in 1911. Officially, it doesn't belong to any country. The territory is reserved for scientific research. Mining and military activities are banned.

Antarctica

The **South Pole** is located roughly in the center of the antarctic continent, on a layer of ice that is about 1,700 feet (2,700 m) thick.

Mount Vinson is 16,050 feet (4,892 m) high and is the highest peak in Antarctica.

In 2010 a new species of **yeti crab** was discovered in the waters of Antarctica. It is 6 inches (15 cm) long and looks like it has blonde hair.

The pale **Ningen** is an imaginary creature that is supposedly part whale, part human.

The tiny **Trinity Church** is one of the eight churches in Antarctica.

The **snowmobile** was the first land vehicle to reach the South Pole, during the Trans-Antarctic Expedition of 1958, which crossed the continent in 99 days.

The **Neumayer III Station** off the antarctic coast was painted red and white to help it stand out from the ice.

The **Drygalski Mountains** are made up of pointed peaks and **nunataks**, rocky islands that come out of glaciers.

Sea spiders that live in the Antarctic are larger than the ones that live in warm waters.

Large **cargo planes** link Antarctica to the rest of the world. There are a number of airports on the continent.

Many modern **polar tents** are similar to those used by the first explorers. They are shaped like pyramids to prevent the snow from building on top of them.

Modern antarctic explorers are scientists who often have to carry out physical tasks like **rappelling** down rocks.

The first explorers on Antarctica had to tow everything on **skis**.

Today, **sleds** made of wood, leather, and rope like the ones used during the first antarctic expeditions are rarely used.

The **emperor penguin** can only be found in Antarctica. It is an extra-ordinary bird that swims like a fish and lives in temperatures of −40°F (−40°C) for months without eating.

The **elephant seal** that lives in Antarctica is as big as its name suggests. It weighs as much as five cows and is the biggest carnivore in the world.

The **leopard seal** has black spots and likes to spend most of its time alone.

Some evidence leads scientists to believe that 500 million years ago an asteroid impact may have caused the large crater beneath the ice in **Wilkes Land**.

The **Mount Erebus** volcano has a lava lake inside of it that continuously puffs smoke.

Dinosaurs like the **Cryolophosaurus** lived on Antarctica 190 million years ago when the continent was closer to the equator.

The **Concept Ice Vehicle** is a cross between a between an airplane and a sled.

Nine out of ten **icebergs** that break off of polar glaciers are in Antarctica. Some are hundreds of miles long.

The **tardigrade** (water bear) is a microscopic animal that can live in temperatures of −328°F (−200°C).

The **southern lights**, like the northern ones, occur when a stream of energy from the sun enters the Earth and "ignites" the gases in our atmosphere.

In Antarctica the **midnight sun** can be seen in winter, when the Earth is tilted so the continent is facing the sun for six months.

Antarctica was sighted for the first time in 1820 by a Russian ship called **Vostok**, but it took another 75 years before an expedition led by Norwegian explorer Roald Amundsen landed on the continent.

The **orca** is sociable and "talks" a lot with other orcas, which makes it very good at hunting seals, dolphins, and even whales in groups.

Icebergs are often shaped like strange **arches** because the center tends to dissolve first, where the temperature is higher.

World Flags

Europe

NORTHERN EUROPE

ICELAND

DENMARK

NORWAY

SWEDEN

FINLAND

LITHUANIA

LATVIA

ESTONIA

UNITED KINGDOM

IRELAND

WESTERN EUROPE

PORTUGAL

SPAIN

ANDORRA

PRINCIPALITY OF MONACO

FRANCE

LUXEMBOURG

BELGIUM

NETHERLANDS

GERMANY

AUSTRIA

LIECHTENSTEIN

SWITZERLAND

ITALY

SAN MARINO

EASTERN EUROPE

VATICAN CITY

MALTA

SLOVENIA

CROATIA

SERBIA

MONTENEGRO

 KOSOVO

 BOSNIA AND HERZEGOVINA

 MACEDONIA

 ALBANIA

 GREECE

CYPRUS

 BULGARIA

 ROMANIA

 MOLDOVA

 HUNGARY

 CZECH REPUBLIC

 SLOVAKIA

 POLAND

 BELARUS

 UKRAINE

 RUSSIA (EUROPEAN)

 TURKEY (EUROPEAN)

Asia

NORTHERN ASIA AND KAZAKHSTAN

 RUSSIA (ASIAN)

 KAZAKHSTAN

 MONGOLIA

CENTRAL ASIA, THE NEAR EAST, AND INDIA

 TURKEY (ASIAN)

 NORTHERN CYPRUS

SYRIA

 LEBANON

 ISRAEL

 STATE OF PALESTINE

 JORDAN

 SAUDI ARABIA

YEMEN

 OMAN

 UNITED ARAB EMIRATES

 QATAR

 BAHRAIN

 KUWAIT

 IRAQ

 GEORGIA

 ARMENIA

 AZERBAIJAN

 IRAN

 AFGHANISTAN

 TURKMENISTAN

 UZBEKISTAN

 KYRGYZSTAN

 TAJIKISTAN

 PAKISTAN

 INDIA

 SRI LANKA

EASTERN ASIA

 NEPAL

 BHUTAN

 BANGLADESH

 CHINA

 TAIWAN

 NORTH KOREA

 SOUTH KOREA

 JAPAN

 MALDIVES

 MYANMAR

 THAILAND

 LAOS

 CAMBODIA

 VIETNAM

 PHILIPPINES

 MALAYSIA

 BRUNEI

 SINGAPORE

 INDONESIA

EAST TIMOR

Africa

NORTH AFRICA

CANARY ISLANDS

MOROCCO

ALGERIA

TUNISIA

LIBYA

EGYPT

SUDAN

ERITREA

DJIBOUTI

SOMALIA

KENYA

SEYCHELLES

ETHIOPIA

SOUTH SUDAN

CHAD

NIGERIA

MALI

WESTERN SAHARA

MAURITANIA

CAPE VERDE

SENEGAL

THE GAMBIA

GUINEA-BISSAU

GUINEA

SIERRA LEONE

LIBERIA

IVORY COAST

BURKINA FASO

GHANA

TOGO

SOUTHERN AFRICA

BENIN

NIGER

CAMEROON

CENTRAL AFRICAN
REPUBLIC

EQUATORIAL GUINEA

SÃO TOMÉ
AND PRÍNCIPE

GABON

REPUBLIC OF THE CONGO

DEMOCRATIC REPUBLIC OF THE CONGO

RWANDA

BURUNDI

UGANDA

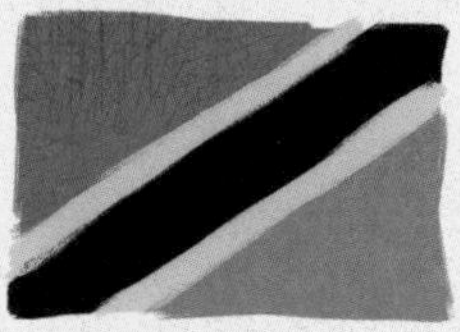

TANZANIA

COMOROS

MAURITIUS

MADAGASCAR

MOZAMBIQUE

MALAWI

ZIMBABWE

ZAMBIA

ANGOLA

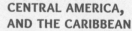

SAINT HELENA (UK)

NAMIBIA

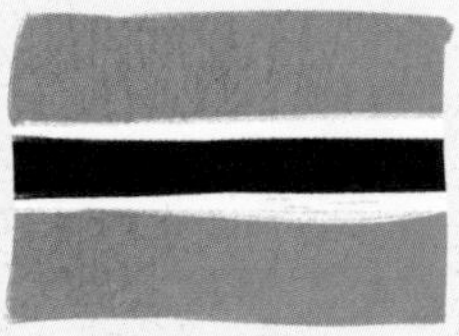

BOTSWANA

SOUTH AFRICA

LESOTHO

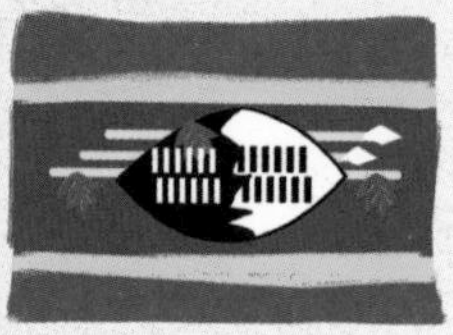

SWAZILAND

The Americas

CANADA, ALASKA, AND GREENLAND

CANADA

ALASKA

GREENLAND (DENMARK)

UNITED STATES OF AMERICA

UNITED STATES OF AMERICA

UK TERRITORY

BERMUDA

CENTRAL AMERICA, AND THE CARIBBEAN

MEXICO

GUATEMALA

BELIZE

HONDURAS

EL SALVADOR

NICARAGUA

COSTA RICA

 PANAMÁ

 BAHAMAS

 CUBA

 CAYMAN ISLANDS (UK)

 JAMAICA

 TURKS AND CAICOS ISLANDS (UK)

 HAITI

 DOMINICAN REPUBLIC

 PUERTO RICO (US)

 BRITISH VIRGIN ISLANDS (UK)

 US VIRGIN ISLANDS (US)

 ANGUILLA (UK)

 SAINT KITTS AND NEVIS

 ANTIGUA AND BARBUDA

 MONTSERRAT (UK)

 GUADELOUPE (FR)

 DOMINICA

 MARTINIQUE (FR)

 BONAIRE (NL)

 SAINT LUCIA

 SAINT VINCENT AND THE GRENADINES

 BARBADOS

 TRINIDAD AND TOBAGO

 ARUBA

SOUTH AMERICA

 CURAÇAO

 GRENADA

 COLOMBIA

 VENEZUELA

 GUYANA

 SURINAME

 FRENCH GUIANA (FR)

 ECUADOR

 GALÁPAGOS ISLANDS (ECUADOR)

 PERÚ

 BOLIVIA

 BRAZIL

 URUGUAY

 PARAGUAY

 ARGENTINA

 CHILE

 FALKLAND ISLANDS (UK)

 SOUTH GEORGIA AND THE SOUTH SANDWICH ISLANDS (UK)

Oceania

AUSTRALIA, PAPUA NEW GUINEA, AND NEW ZEALAND

PACIFIC ISLANDS

AUSTRALIA

TASMANIA
(AUS)

NEW ZEALAND

PAPUA NEW GUINEA

PALAU

FEDERATED STATES
OF MICRONESIA

NORTHERN MARIANA
ISLANDS (US)

GUAM (US)

BONIN ISLANDS
(JAPAN)

MARSHALL ISLANDS

NAURU

SOLOMON ISLANDS

CORAL SEA ISLANDS
(AUS)

TUVALU

WALLIS AND FUTUNA
(FR)

VANUATU

NEW CALEDONIA
(FR)

FIJI

TONGA

SAMOA

TOKELAU (NZ)

AMERICAN SAMOA
(US)

KIRIBATI

NIUE (NZ)

COOK ISLANDS

HAWAII (US)

FRENCH POLYNESIA
(FR)

PITCAIRN ISLANDS
(UK)

EASTER ISLAND
(CHILE)

JUAN FERNÁNDEZ
ISLANDS (CHILE)

PALMYRA ATOLL
(US)

Index

Abbreviations

AUS = Australia
FR = France
NL = Netherlands
NZ = New Zealand
UK = United Kingdom
US = United States